Spanish

AMONG AMIGOS
PHRASEBOOK

Conversation for the Socially Adventurous

SECOND EDITION

Nuria

New York   Chicago   San Francisco   Lisbon   London   Madrid   Mexico City
Milan   New Delhi   San Juan   Seoul   Singapore   Sydney   Toronto

3 4 5 6 7 8 9 10 11 12 13 14 15 16   QFR/QFR   1 9 8 7 6 5 4

ISBN   978-0-07-175415-6
MHID   0-07-175415-6

Library of Congress Cataloging-in-Publication Data

Agulló, Nuria.
      Spanish among amigos phrasebook / Nuria Agullo. — 2nd ed.
          p.   cm.
      English and Spanish.
      ISBN 0-07-175415-6 (alk. paper)
      1. Spanish language—Conversation and phrase books—English.   I. Title.

   PC4121.A273   2010
   468.3′421—dc22   2010037336

Interior design by Village Typographers, Inc.
Interior illustrations by Jorge Méndez-Germain

McGraw-Hill books are available at special quantity discounts to use as premiums and sales promotions or for use in corporate training programs. To contact a representative, please e-mail us at bulksales@mcgraw-hill.com.

This book is printed on acid-free paper.

Contents

Acknowledgments

First of all, I want to thank my ingenious editor, Garret Lemoi, for talking me into doing this phrasebook. Thanks, Garret, for your enthusiasm and encouragement! Thanks also to my agent, Ed Knappman, for being there when needed, and various phone chats when your support, patience, and mellow baritone voice did wonders. I also feel lucky to have dealt with Charlie Fisher, who orchestrated the book's production. Cheers, Charlie, you're a real class act. As for the core support team—all *amigos*—their identities will be protected (no full names here), and they will remain fabulously incognito. Here goes . . .

Thanks, Juan, for your beautiful editing job. Thanks, Hugo, for your pithy cutting-edge suggestions. Thanks, Marino, Nenorra, and Oscar, for making the Spanish even leaner and meaner. Thanks, Jorge, for your flexibility and flair on the illustrations. Thanks, Jani Bani, for being a fab all-around consultant. Thanks, Juan José, for wading through the word bank so carefully. Thanks, Duquesa D'Ortera and Lotte, for your save-the-day input on American slang. Thanks, Fran, for being the bridge to Latin America. Ditto Luis, my *cono sur* consultant. And *un millón de gracias*, Chuchi, Javi, John, José, Lourdes, Mandi, Marina, Papi, Pas, Rocío, Silos, Stevie, Sweetums, and Trisha for your help, interest, and encouragement. Last but not least, *mucha gracia* (not typos—they zap the final "s" down here) to all my *amigos* in Cáceres who have made my semi-sabbatical here a real treat.

Introduction

First of all, as you've probably guessed, this is not your basic Spanish phrasebook. That is, if you're looking for phrases to deal with waiters, sales clerks, and hotel receptionists, you've come to the wrong place. This is not about survival Spanish. We assume you can survive. We also assume you're interested in something more than getting by.

This phrasebook is about really conversing in Spanish. And yes, it's written with a special type of person in mind—someone who's already got a little Spanish under his or her belt and who's more into the living culture than being carted around to see the sights. In other words, all you adventurous souls who want to strike out beyond textbook or survival mode, and start really communicating with people.

So how does this phrasebook work? Basically it gives you the tools you need to carry on a conversation. Each unit zooms in on a key social function: greeting people, breaking the ice, relaying news and gossip, giving your opinion, and so on. Apart from ready-to-go phrases that'll get you sounding like a native, you'll also find grammar pointers, insights into Spanish culture, notes on idioms and slang, and tips on avoiding common blunders.

Along the way, you'll also be exposed to real-life conversations in Spanish among *amigos*. Enter Pepa and Pili, along with their friend Lola and Mark, an American whose Spanish doesn't quite measure up. You may have already met this duo from Madrid in *Spanish Among Amigos*, a hands-on vocabulary builder that later gave rise to the idea for this phrasebook. We've toned down the dialogues here to make them a little more accessible, but for those of you who aren't familiar with the original *Spanish Among Amigos* and are up for a bit more of a challenge after this, we recommend that you check it out.

That's all, folks! We hope this phrasebook not only opens up new horizons, but also has you chuckling along the way. And best of luck on your Spanish odyssey. May you make many new *amigos*!

How to Use This Phrasebook

Here are a few tips that will help you get the most out of this book. Follow them, and you're in business!

Learn and Improvise

This book is not intended to be used as a script. Any conversation needs a good dose of spontaneity and improvisation. By all means keep this book handy for on-the-spot consultation, but we recommend that you try to learn and assimilate the phrases you think you'll need ahead of time.

Pick and Choose

As in English, there are many ways in Spanish to say hello, goodbye, give your opinion, offer advice, and so on. We've tried to make this phrasebook as comprehensive as possible, and you'll see that the lists of phrases are quite long and varied. Our recommendation: think of these lists as aisles in a language supermarket. It's good to see and be familiar with what's available, but you end up getting just one or two items from each aisle at any one time. Do the same here. Pick one or two phrases from each list to actively use: the shortest phrase, the one you like the look or sound of, or the one that's easiest for you to remember.

Observe the Natives

Ready-to-go phrases are fine, but it always helps to see them in context and observe how native Spanish speakers use them. That's why we've kicked off each unit with a dialogue featuring some of the unit's key phrases "in action." The dialogues, which are accompanied by "natural" English translations, will help give you a feel for the spirit and rhythm of everyday Spanish.

Brush Up on Your Grammar

Though you don't need perfect grammar to communicate, brushing up on the basics doesn't hurt. To this end, we've sprinkled *grammar flashes* throughout the units, with brief pointers and reminders on those structures you'll need to know. We've also included a Grammar Bank at the end of the book to consult when you have questions or doubts. This contains the main building blocks you'll need to carry on a conversation among *amigos*.

Handle with Care!

This phrasebook also includes common idioms and slang, which we've flagged with emoticons (see "Abbreviations and Symbols Used in This Phrasebook"). Use these words and phrases to pepper your speech and give it a little added oomph. Be careful, though! Idioms and slang sometimes sound forced or inappropriate when used by nonnative speakers. Be particularly careful about how and when you use *hard slang* (words flagged by a surprised face). Our advice: go with it if you feel comfortable. When in doubt, don't.

Don't Be Fooled!

Yes, there are lots of false friends, or false cognates, out there—that is, words that look similar in Spanish and English, but have completely different meanings. We've highlighted common words that may be misleading in *false friend alerts*, to help you avoid misunderstandings and blunders on this front. We've also included *verb alerts* that zoom in on verbs that can cause confusion.

Get into the Spirit of Things

Language is also culture, and every culture has its traditions, quirks, and views. To give you a better grasp and get you into the spirit of things, we've inserted *culture flashes* throughout this phrasebook. Here you'll find comments on aspects of Spanish culture, particularly customs, views and/or attitudes that differ from those of English-speaking countries.

Flip to That Word

Don't know or can't remember a word? Look it up in the Word Bank at the end of the book. Here you'll find everyday words related to different topics. The Word Bank has been broken down into twenty categories, each containing various subheadings, to help you quickly find the word you need.

Just Say It!

Since we assume most of you are familiar with the way Spanish is written and sounds, we've opted not to include the phonetic spelling next to each phrase or entry. We have, however, provided a pronunciation guide at the beginning of the book to consult if you have any doubts about pronunciation or word stress. This also includes a key to saying the alphabet in Spanish, to help you understand words being spelled to you, or else to spell a name or word yourself.

Get Creative

Forgotten an expression or aren't sure how to say something? (And, darn, you left this book at home!) Take the plunge, and do the best you can. Get creative. Take an English word, and give it Spanish pronunciation. If it's an adjective, tack on an *o* or *a* at the end. Since many English words have Latin roots, you'll hit the bull's-eye half the time. And when you don't, proceed to plan B. Use gestures, tone, body language, humor. Whip out any word that comes to mind. In the worst-case scenario, you'll entertain your *amigos* and they'll love you for it.

Keep at It!

This phrasebook is simply a tool. It will help you, but you have to do the legwork and keep at it. Remember also that striking out in another language is fun but can be defeating at moments. Take things one step at a time, and don't expect miracles overnight. Most important of all, stick with it and don't give up. At moments you may feel lost, but little by little, you'll pick up new phrases, and understand more and more of what people are saying. And one fine day you may realize you don't need this book anymore, and can give it to a friend . . .

Abbreviations and Symbols Used in This Phrasebook

The following abbreviations and symbols appear throughout this phrasebook:

@ *o* or *a* ending of an adjective or noun. When you see a word ending in this symbol, it represents both its masculine (-*o*) and feminine (-*a*) forms.

amig@ amigo, amiga

This cyber symbol is becoming popular in Spain (since it looks like an *a* inside an *o*) as a way to indicate masculine and feminine forms of the same word, and we've decided to follow suit here.

@s *os* or *as* ending of an adjective or noun. This represents the plural masculine (-*os*) and feminine (-*as*) forms of adjectives and nouns.

amig@s amigos, amigas

☺ colloquial expression or idiom (used by people of all ages)

😀 "soft" slang (popular words and expressions used a lot by young people and accepted by everybody)

😈 "hard" slang (popular words and expressions that are potentially offensive and should be restricted to use among *amigos*)

[LA] word or expression used in most of Latin America

[SP] word or expression used only in Spain

sb somebody

st something

Pronunciation Guide

Spanish is relatively easy to pronounce. It has only five vowel sounds (there are around 20 in English, including diphthongs), and many of the consonants sound like their English counterparts. Also, there are only a few pronunciation rules, and once you know them, you're in business. As for that rolled *r*, if you can do it, fabulous. If not, no sweat. Just use the English *r*, and you'll be understood.

Vowels

The five Spanish vowel sounds are very similar to the English vowel sounds below, though a little purer and crisper.

A   like the *ah* you say at the dentist's
E   like the *e* in *bet*
I   like the *ee* in *meet,* but less drawn out
O   like the *o* in *for*
U   like the *oo* in *cool*

Consonants

These consonants are pronounced pretty much like their English equivalents: **F, K, L, M, N, P, S, T, X, Y.**

The rest are pronounced as follows:

B   softer than the English *b*. (*tip*: keep your lips slightly closed—but not pressed together as you do with the English *b*)

C   before *a, o, u,* or a consonant (e.g., *cama*): a hard *c* as in *cat*. Before *e* or *i* (e.g., *cena*):
    [LA] a soft *c* as in *receive*
    [SP] a *th* sound as in *thin*

D   when it's the first letter of a word (e.g., *decir*): like *d* in *dog*. Elsewhere (e.g., *adorar*): like *th* in *that*

G   before *a, o,* and *u* (e.g., *gato*): like *g* in *gate*. Before *e* or *i* (e.g., *gente*):
    [LA] like *h* in *house*
    [SP] a harsh, guttural sound like *ch* in the Scottish *loch*

H   silent

J [LA] like **h** in **house**
[SP] a harsh, guttural sound like **ch** in the Scottish **loch**

LL like **y** in **yes**

Ñ like **ni** in **onion**

Q like **k** in **key**; note that **q** is always followed by a silent **u**, and is only combined with **e** (e.g., **que, quedar**) or **i** (e.g., **quien, quitar**)

R single **r** (e.g., **venir**): rolled **r** sound
initial **r** or double **r** (e.g., **ropa, perro**): strongly rolled **r** sound

V the same sound as the Spanish **b**

Z [LA] like **s** in **send**   [SP] like **th** in **thin**

Stress

Words in Spanish have the stress on the second-to-last syllable

estupendo   estudiante   casa   hermano

Unless . . .

- a word ends in a consonant other than **n** or **s**. In this case the stress is on the last syllable.

español   estudiar   venir

- the word has a written accent. In this case, the stress is on the accented vowel.

café   estación   pacífico

The Alphabet

We're including this, as it could come in handy for spelling words, including names of people and places.

The vowel sounds in the alphabet have been represented as follows:

ah   Spanish *a* (that dentist "ah")

eh   Spanish *e* (like *e* in *bet*)

ee   Spanish *i* (like *ee* in *meet*)

oh   Spanish *o* (like *o* in *for*)

oo   Spanish *u* (like *oo* in *cool*)

In letters containing more than one syllable, the stress is on the syllable in italics.

A	ah
B	beh
C	[LA] seh
	[SP] theh
CH	cheh
D	deh
E	eh
F	*eh*-feh
G	heh
H	*ah*-cheh
I	ee
J	*hoh*-tah
K	kah
L	*eh*-leh
LL	*eh*-yeh
M	*eh*-meh
N	*eh*-neh
Ñ	*eh*-nee-eh
O	oh
P	peh
Q	koo
R	*eh*-reh
S	*eh*-seh
T	teh
U	oo
V	*oo*-veh
W	*oo*-veh doh-bleh
X	*eh*-kees
Y	ee-gree-*eh*-gah
Z	[LA] *seh*-tah
	[SP] *theh*-tah

Spanish
AMONG AMIGOS
PHRASEBOOK

1

Meeting and Greeting

It's been a while since Pepa and Pili last saw each other. They run into each other on the street . . .

Pili   **¡Hola**, Pepa!

Pepa   **¡Hombre**, Pili! *(Se dan dos besos.)* **¿Qué tal?**

Pili   **Estupendamente. ¿Y tú?**

Pepa   **Bien. Sin novedades.**

Pili   Bueno, **¡cuánto tiempo!** Pensé que habías desaparecido del mapa.

Pepa   Lo siento, es que he estado muy liada.

Pili   No pasa nada. Mira, **te presento a** Mark, un amigo de Estados Unidos. Estamos haciendo un intercambio.

Pepa   **Hola. Encantada.**

Mark   **Hola. ¿Qué tal?** *(Se dan dos besos.)*

Pepa   ¿Vives aquí en Madrid?

Mark   Sí, voy a estar un tiempo. Quiero mejorar mi español.

Pepa   ¡Ah! Pues con Pili vas a aprender mucho, ya verás.

Pili   ¡Ja, ja, ja! Desde luego. Oye, Pepa, ahora tenemos que irnos, pero **a ver si nos vemos pronto.**

Pepa   Venga, y así **nos ponemos al día.**

Pili   Estupendo. **Hablamos pronto.** *(Se dan dos besos.)*

Pepa   **¡Chao! ¡Pasadlo bien!**

Mark   **¡Hasta luego!**

Pili	Hi, Pepa!
Pepa	Hey, Pili! (*They kiss on both cheeks.*) **How are you?**
Pili	Great. How about you?
Pepa	Good. Not much happening.
Pili	Wow, **it's been a while!** I thought you'd fallen off the face of the earth.
Pepa	I'm sorry, I've been really tied up.
Pili	Don't worry. Hey, **this is** Mark, a friend from the United States. We're doing a language exchange.
Pepa	**Hi. Nice to meet you.**
Mark	**Hi. How are you?** (*They kiss on both cheeks.*)
Pepa	Do you live here in Madrid?
Mark	Yes, I'm going to be here for a while. I want to improve my Spanish.
Pepa	Oh! Well, you're going to learn a lot with Pili, just wait and see.
Pili	Ha, ha! Of course. Hey, Pepa, we've got to go now, but **let's get together soon.**
Pepa	OK, and that way **we can catch up.**
Pili	Great. **Talk to you soon.** (*They kiss on both cheeks.*)
Pepa	**Ciao! Have fun!**
Mark	**See you!**

Saying Hello

¡Hola!	Hello!/Hi!
¿Cómo estás?	How are you?
¿Qué tal (estás)?	How are you?
¿Cómo andas? ☺	How's it going?
¿Qué hay? ☺	What's up?/What's new?
¡Hombre! ☺ [SP]	Hey!/Well hello! (*used when you run into or hear from someone unexpectedly; hombre here is an exclamation of surprise and is used with both men and women*)
¿Cómo lo llevas? ☻ [SP]	How's it going?/How are you doing?
¿Qué pasa? ☻	What's up?/What's happening?
¡Buenos días!	Good morning!

And If It's Been a While

¿Qué tal todo?	How's everything?
¿Cómo te va (la vida)?	How's it going?/How's life?
¿Qué es de tu vida?	How's life?/What have you been up to?
¡Cuánto tiempo!	It's been a while!/Long time no see!
¡Hace siglos que no nos vemos!	It's been ages!
Pensé que habías desaparecido del mapa.	I thought you'd fallen off the face of the earth.
Vamos a ponernos al día.	Let's catch up.
A ver cuando nos vemos.	Let's get together sometime.
A ver si nos vemos pronto.	Let's get together soon.
A ver si quedamos pronto.	Let's get together soon.

Aaagh!!!

Yes, **buen@** usually means *good*. But if you use it with the verb *estar* (as opposed to *ser*) and you're referring to a person, it means he or she is hot (i.e., physically attractive). For saying how you are, use the adverb **bien**.

Responding

(Muy) bien.	(Really) good.
Estupendamente.	Great.
Genial.☻	Great.
Fenomenal.☻ [SP]	Fantastic.
Fantástic@.	Fabulous.
No me puedo quejar.	I can't complain.
Tirando.☺ [SP]	Getting by.
Sin novedades.	Not much happening./ No news./Not much.
Regular.	Not so great.
Así, así.	So-so.
(Muy) mal.	Not great.
Jodid@.☹ [SP]	Lousy. (*literally,* fucked; *vulgar, but very common*)
Pésim@.☻ [LA]	Terrible.
Fatal.☻ [SP]	Awful.

Culture Flash • Kissy Wissy

You may have noticed there's a lot of kissing going on in the opening dialogue. Is this normal? Absolutely! In Spain, every time two women or a man and a woman say hello, good-bye, or meet each other for the first time, they lunge at each other's cheeks. This is known as *los dos besos*—"the two kisses"—one on each cheek (though note that in Latin America one kiss is the norm). But a word to the wise: be careful not to overdo it. *Los dos besos* are rarely warm and slurpy. Accepted practice ranges from a perfunctory bob of the head on each side of a person's face to a light brush of the cheeks, with the actual smooch heading out into space. Anything more (that is, full lip-to-cheek contact) conveys strong emotion or else some sexual interest. Men generally smile and nod at each other, with or without a little back-slapping or patting (except with immediate family members, where *los dos besos* is the norm), and shake hands when they meet for the first time. Note, however, that *los dos besos* is also common among gay men and is gaining ground now in Spain among more liberal urban men too.

Asking About a Mutual Friend

¿Cómo está (Pepa)?	How's (Pepa)?
¿Qué tal está (Pili)?	How's (Pili)?
¿Qué sabes de (Lola)?	Any news of (Lola)?
¿Sabes algo de (Luis)?	Any news of (Luis)?
Hace tiempo que no lo/la veo.	It's been a while since I saw him/her.
Hace tiempo que no sé nada de él/ella.	It's been a while since we've been in touch.
Mándale/Dale saludos de mi parte.	Tell him/her I said hello.

Mándale/Dale recuerdos de mi parte. [SP]	Give him/her my regards.
Mándale/Dale un beso de mi parte.	Send him/her my love.

Saying Good-bye

Adiós.	Good-bye.
Chao.☺	Ciao./Bye for now.
Nos vemos.	See you.
Hasta luego.	See you./Bye. *(the most common of the hasta expressions)*
Hasta pronto.	See you soon.
Hasta otra.	See you./Bye. *(when it's someone you don't know well, and you don't know when you'll see him or her again)*
Hasta la próxima.	See you. *(has the idea of "until we meet again")*
Hasta la vista.	See you./Bye. *(similar to hasta otra)*
Hasta ahora. [SP]	See you in a bit. *(when you're coming right back)*
Hasta entonces.	See you then. *(when you've already referred to the next time you'll see each other)*
Hasta (el viernes).	See you (on Friday).
Hasta mañana.	See you tomorrow.
Hablamos pronto.	Let's talk soon.
Estamos en contacto.	Let's be in touch.
¡Buenas noches!	Good night!

Little Extras

¡Que tengas buen viaje!	Have a good trip!
¡Que tengas suerte!	Good luck!
¡Que lo pases bien!	Have a good time!
¡Que te diviertas!	Have fun!/Enjoy yourself!

¡Que descanses!	Get some rest!
¡Que te vaya bien!	Best of luck!/Wish you well!
¡Que te sea leve!☺ [SP]	Take it easy!/Don't sweat it! (*literally,* May it be light for you!)

Short Forms

¡Buen viaje!	Have a good trip!
¡Suerte! *or* ¡Mucha suerte!	Good luck!
¡Pásalo bien!*	Have a good time!
¡Diviértete!*	Have fun!
¡Descansa!*	Get some rest!

Grammar Flash • (Yikes!) The Subjunctive ...

Don't worry if you're not on top of the subjunctive. Most people run into doubts about how and when to use it. Just note that you need it with these *little extras* that begin with *que* when the meaning is *may you . . .* : *may you rest, may you sleep well, may you have a good trip*, etc. Yes, in English this conjures up visions of medieval knights, and you'd just use the imperative (*Get some rest! Sleep well! Have a good trip!*), but in Spanish these expressions are standard fare and don't sound comical or obsolete.

Also, note that if you're talking to more than one person, you'll need the plural form of these expressions. In Spain, the *vosotros* form is used; in Latin America, the *Uds.* form is used. (For the plural forms of the subjunctive, consult pages 141–142 in the Grammar Bank.)

OK, it may seem like a lot to remember when all you want to do is tag on a little extra to your ¡**adiós**! or ¡**hasta luego**! Our recommendation: avoid the subjunctive when you can by sticking to the short forms: ¡**Buen viaje**! ¡**Suerte**! ¡**Pásalo bien**!

---

*For the plural forms, see "Is That an Order?" on page 139 in the Grammar Bank.

Introducing Yourself or a Friend

Hola, soy (Pepa).	Hi, I'm (Pepa).
Hola, me llamo (Pepa).	Hi, my name's (Pepa).
Te presento a (Pili).	This is (Pili).
Éste/Ésta es (Luis/Pili).	This is (Luis/Pili). *(more informal)*
¿Conoces a (Pili)?	Do you know (Pili)?
¿Os conocéis?	Do you know each other?
Hola. ¿Qué tal?	Hi. How are you? *(more informal)*
Encantad@.*	Pleased to meet you.
Mucho gusto.*	Pleased to meet you.

False Friend Alert!

Speaking of friends, watch out for *false friends* (known officially as false cognates), words that look similar in two languages, but have totally different meanings. **Introducir**, for example, means *to insert*, not *to introduce*. So if (heaven forbid!) you were to say **te introduzco a Ana**, you can guess what your friend Ana might think. Remember, when you're introducing people, use **presentar**.

---

*These are also used when you say good-bye to someone you've met for the first time (much like "Nice meeting you.").

On the Spot

A   *You run into Pepa on the street. Fill in the blanks in your conversation.*

Pepa   Hola, ¿qué (1)_____?

Tú   Muy bien. ¿Y tú? ¿Qué es de tu (2)_____?

Pepa   Pues bien. Sin (3)_____.

Tú   Y Pili, ¿cómo (4)_____? ¡Hace (5)_____ que no nos vemos!

Pepa   Pues muy bien. Tan loca como siempre...

Tú   ¡Ja, ja, ja! Pues cuando la veas, por favor dale recuerdos de mi (6)_____.

Pepa   Lo haré. Oye, tengo que irme ahora, pero a ver si nos (7)_____ pronto.

Tú   Estupendo, nos llamamos.

Pepa   ¡Chao! ¡(8)_____ pronto!

B *You run into Pili and Mark a few days later. Fill in the blanks in your conversation.*

Pili   ¡Hola! ¿Cómo estás?

Tú   Muy (1)_____. Y tú, ¿qué tal?

Pili   Genial. Bueno, ¡(2)_____ tiempo!

Tú   Sí, ha sido casi un año.

Pili   ¡Tanto! ¡Madre mía! Oye, te (3)_____ a Mark, un amigo de Estados Unidos.

Mark   Hola. ¿Qué (4)_____?

Tú   Mucho (5)_____. ¿Vives aquí?

Mark   Si, de momento. Quiero mejorar mi español.

Tú   ¿Ah, sí? Pues que te (6)_____ muy bien.

Mark   Gracias.

Pili   Oye, tenemos que irnos ahora, pero ¿hablamos pronto?

Tú   Estupendo. Y nos ponemos al (7)_____.

Pili   Venga, nos llamamos. ¡Chao!

Tú   ¡Adiós! ¡(8)_____ luego!

2

Same Time, Same Place?

A few days later, Pili phones Mark.

Pili	Hola, Mark, soy Pili.
Mark	¡Ah, Pili! ¿Qué tal?
Pili	Bien. Oye, **lo siento, pero no voy a poder quedar** esta tarde.
Mark	¿Cómo? ¿Quedar? ¿Quedar dónde?
Pili	Quedar contigo, tonto.
Mark	¿Quedar *conmigo*?
Pili	Sí, Mark. ¿No te acuerdas que hoy íbamos a **quedar para tomar un café**?
Mark	¡Ah, sí! Es verdad. Ahora entiendo.
Pili	**Es que me ha surgido algo.**
Mark	**No te preocupes. Lo dejamos para otro día.**
Pili	**¿No te importa?**
Mark	**En absoluto. Hoy me viene un poco mal a mí también.**
Pili	**¿Y si nos vemos mañana?**
Mark	Bien. ¿**Te viene bien** a las seis de la tarde?
Pili	**Perfecto. ¿Quedamos donde siempre?**
Mark	¿En el Café Comercial? De acuerdo.
Pili	¡Ah!, y otra cosa. El sábado hago una fiesta en casa. ¿**Te apuntas**?
Mark	¿Cómo?
Pili	**¿Puedes venir? ¿Cuento contigo?**
Mark	¡Ah! Sí, por supuesto. **Cuenta conmigo.**
Pili	Estupendo. Pues nada, **nos vemos** mañana, ¿vale?
Mark	Muy bien. Hasta entonces.
Pili	Chao.

Pili	Hi, Mark, it's Pili.
Mark	Hey, Pili. How's it going?
Pili	Good. Listen, **I'm sorry, but I'm not going to be able to make it** [literally, *stay*] this afternoon.
Mark	What? Stay? Stay where?
Pili	Meet up [literally, *stay*] with you, silly.
Mark	Stay *with me*?
Pili	Yes, Mark. Don't you remember we were going **to meet** [literally, *stay*] **for a coffee** today?
Mark	Oh yeah! That's right. I understand now.
Pili	**I'm sorry, but something's come up.**
Mark	**Don't worry. We can do it another day.**
Pili	**You don't mind?**
Mark	Not at all. Today's not great for me either.
Pili	**How about getting together tomorrow?**
Mark	Fine. **How about in the afternoon**, around six o'clock?
Pili	**Great. Same place as always?**
Mark	The Café Comercial? **Fine.**
Pili	Oh, and one more thing. I'm having a party at my place on Saturday. **Will you come?** [literally, *sign up*]
Mark	Huh?
Pili	Can you come? **Can I count you in?**
Mark	Oh! Yes, of course. **Count me in.**
Pili	Great. Well then, so **I'll see you** tomorrow, OK?
Mark	Great. See you then.
Pili	Bye.

Suggesting a Plan

¿Por qué no...?	Why don't . . . ?
quedamos☺ mañana	we meet up tomorrow
tomamos un café	we get together for a coffee
vienes a comer a casa	you come over for lunch [SP]/ dinner [LA]
¿Te apetece...? [SP]	Do you feel like . . . ?
¿Te provoca...? [LA]	Do you feel like . . . ?
quedar☺ esta tarde	meeting up this evening
ir al cine	going to the movies
tomar algo por ahí	going out for a bite to eat/ a drink
¿Quieres...?	Do you want . . . ?
ir al concierto	to go to the concert
ir a la exposición	to go to the exhibition
salir esta noche	to go out tonight
¿Qué te parece si...?	How about . . . ?
¿Y si...?	How about . . . ?
quedamos☺ por mi zona	meeting up in my neighborhood
vamos al cine	going to the movies
cenamos por ahí	going out for dinner
Podríamos...	We could . . .
ir al concierto	go to the concert
salir a cenar	go out for dinner
quedar☺ más tarde	meet up later
¿Vamos...?	Shall we go . . . ?
a la exposición mañana	to the exhibition tomorrow
a tomar algo por ahí	out for a bite to eat/a drink
de excursión el sábado	on a day trip on Saturday
¿Te apuntas?☺	Are you on?
¿Te animas?	Are you game?
¿Cuento contigo?	Can I count you in?/Will you come?

Slang Flash • *quedar* and *apuntarse*

quedar☺ [SP]

Yes, this means *to stay* or *remain*. But it's also used a lot informally to refer to plans and getting together. **Quedar (con alguien)** doesn't have a real English equivalent, but it roughly means *to arrange to meet (someone)*.

¿Cómo quedamos?	When and where shall we meet?
He quedado con Lola más tarde.	I'm seeing Lola later.
Lo siento, no puedo, he quedado.	I'm sorry, I can't, I'm busy/ I've got plans.

apuntarse☺ [SP]

This means *to sign up* or *join* (a gym, a club, a course, etc.) But, speaking informally, **apuntarse** means *to be on for something* (generally, a group plan or event), that is, to want to participate or go along.

Vamos de excursión el sábado. ¿Te apuntas?	We're going on a day trip on Saturday. Are you on?/ Want to come?
Sí, me apunto.	Yes, count me in./Yes, I'm on.

Deciding on a Time

¿Qué haces esta tarde?	What are you doing this afternoon?
¿Vas a hacer algo esta tarde?	Doing anything this afternoon?
¿Qué planes tienes esta tarde?	What are you up to this afternoon?
¿Tienes planes esta tarde?	Have you got any plans for this afternoon?

¿Estás ocupad@ esta tarde?	Are you busy this afternoon?
¿Estás libre esta tarde?	Are you free this afternoon?
¿Cuándo...?	When . . . ?
¿A qué hora...?	What time . . . ?
quedamos☺	shall we meet
te viene bien	is good for you
¿Quedamos☺...?	Shall we meet . . . ?
mañana	tomorrow
a las ocho	at eight o'clock
¿Te viene bien...?	Is . . . good for you?
a las nueve	nine o'clock
pasado mañana	the day after tomorrow
(Mañana/el viernes),	How's (tomorrow/Friday) look
¿cómo lo tienes? [SP]	for you?
Nos vemos...	See you . . .
a las cinco	at five o'clock
esta tarde	this evening

Key Phrase • venir(le) bien/mal

This expression is used to indicate that a plan or situation suits you or is "good" (that is, convenient or welcome). **Venir(le) mal** means the opposite—that is, that a plan or situation is inconvenient or unwelcome.

¿Te viene bien a las ocho?	Is eight o'clock good for you?
Me viene mal el viernes.	Friday's not good for me.
¿Y si quedamos el sábado?	How about Saturday?
Me viene bien tener a Pili en casa. Así practico el español.	It's good having Pili around the house. That way I can practice my Spanish.
Le vendrá bien tomar unos días de descanso.	A few days' rest will do him good.

Deciding on a Place

¿Dónde quedamos☺?	Where shall we meet?
¿Quedamos☺...?	Shall we meet . . . ?
delante del cine	in front of the movie theater
donde siempre	at the usual place
¿Te viene bien...?	Is . . . OK by you?
pasar por mi casa	coming by my place
(quedar) por el centro	(meeting) downtown
¿Paso por tu casa?	Shall I come by your place?
¿Te recojo en tu casa?	Shall I pick you up at your place?
Nos vemos...	See you . . .
allí	there
en casa de Pepa	at Pepa's place

Responding
Affirmative

De acuerdo.	OK.
Estupendo.	Great.
¡Hecho!	Agreed!/OK!
Me parece bien.	Sounds good.
Muy bien.	Fine./OK.
OK.☻ [LA]	OK.
Perfecto.	Fine./Great.
Cuenta conmigo.	Count me in./I'll be there.
Vale.☻ [SP]	OK.
Venga.☻ [SP]	Great./OK.
Ya.☺ [LA]	All right./Fine.
Sí, me viene bien (hoy).	Yes, (today) is fine with me.
Sí, no me viene mal (esta tarde).	Yes, (this afternoon/evening) isn't bad for me.
Me vendría mejor...	. . . would be better for me.
Prefiero/Preferiría...	I'd rather . . .
mañana	tomorrow
a las ocho y media	(at) eight-thirty
por la Plaza Mayor	(around) the Plaza Mayor

Culture Flash • Plan? What Plan?

Although this unit is about making plans, note that plans in most Spanish-speaking countries need to be taken with a grain of salt. Yes, in Latin cultures spontaneity reigns: friends "forget," things come up, and day-to-day life follows the dictates of momentary impulses, shifting moods, chance encounters, and spur-of-the-moment decisions.

So shelve your diary, hang loose, and take heart in the fact that this spontaneity principle can work in your favor too. That is, you too can ignore or "forget" that plan to meet up with Paco for coffee, if a long-lost friend suddenly calls and wants to get together, or you just aren't up to seeing Paco, who you adore, but whose company can be a little demanding. And if Paco calls from the café wondering where you are (highly unlikely, as he's probably "forgotten" the plan too, if you haven't already called it off that morning on the phone), slip into Latin mode. This is your cue to feign amnesia. "¿Plan? ¿Qué plan?"

Negative

Lo siento, pero...	I'm sorry, but . . .
Me encantaría, pero...	I'd love to, but . . .
he quedado	I've got plans/I'm busy
hoy lo tengo complicado	today's difficult for me
me viene mal hoy	today's not good for me
me ha surgido algo	something's come up
no puedo	I can't
no voy a poder quedar hoy	I'm not going to be able to make it today
me es imposible hoy	today's impossible for me
No me apetece mucho. [SP]	I really don't feel like it.
Es un poco caro.	It's a little expensive.
Está un poco lejos.	It's a little far.

Opting Out · Es que...

ES QUE...ESTOY MUY OCUPADA

So you want to opt out of a plan and need to make an excuse or offer an explanation. Here's a common lead-in that will do the job. *Es que...* literally means *It's that . . .* , though the English equivalent would be *I'm sorry . . . , I can't . . .* or *The thing is . . .*

Es que me ha surgido algo.	I'm sorry, something's come up.
Es que hoy tengo un examen.	I can't, I have an exam today.
Es que tengo que hacer un recado.	The thing is I have an errand to run.
Es que mañana madrugo.	The thing is I have to get up early tomorrow.

Useful Phrases for Canceling Plans

Lo dejamos para otro día.	Let's take a rain check.
¿No te importa?	You don't mind?/Is that OK with you?
En absoluto.	Not at all.

No importa.
No pasa nada.☺ }   Don't worry./Never mind.
No te preocupes.

Hoy/mañana/esta semana...   Today/tomorrow/this week . . .
   también me viene mal   is bad for me too
   también lo tengo complicado   is difficult for me too
   tampoco me viene bien   isn't good for me either

On the Spot

A   *You call up Pili to arrange to meet. Fill in the blanks in your conversation.*

Pili   ¿Sí?

Tú   Hola, Pili.

Pili   ¡Hombre! ¿Qué tal?

Tú   Bien. Oye, ¿qué planes (1) _____ esta tarde?

Pili   Ninguno, de momento. ¿Por qué?

Tú   ¿Te (2) _____ tomar algo por ahí?

Pili   Venga. ¿Cuándo (3) _____?

Tú   ¿Te (4) _____ bien a las ocho?

Pili   Sí, perfecto. ¿Quedamos donde (5) _____?

Tú   Vale.

Pili   Genial. Oye, y no hagas planes para el sábado.

Tú   ¿Por qué?

Pili   Es mi cumpleaños, y hago una fiesta. ¿Te (6) _____?

Tú   Por supuesto. Cuenta (7) _____.

Pili   Estupendo. Pues nada, nos vemos esta tarde.

Tú   Hasta entonces.

B *Pili calls you back two hours later. Fill in the blanks in your conversation.*

Pili Oye, lo siento, pero no voy a poder (1)_____ esta tarde.

Tú No te (2)_____.

Pili Lo siento de verdad. (3)_____ _____tengo mucho trabajo.

Tú No (4)_____ nada. Lo (5)_____ para otro día.

Pili ¿No te (6)_____?

Tú En absoluto. En todo caso, nos vemos el sábado en tu fiesta, ¿no?

Pili Pues sí. ¡Allí te espero!

3

Breaking the Ice

Mark chats with a woman at Pili's party.

Mark	Perdón, **¿tienes fuego?**
Lola	Lo siento, no fumo.
Mark	No importa. Por cierto, me llamo Mark.
Lola	Yo Lola. **¿De dónde eres?**
Mark	**Soy americano, de Chicago.**
Lola	¡Ah!, eso explica ese acento.
Mark	Y **¿conoces a Pili desde hace mucho?**
Lola	**De toda la vida.** Fíjate, **la conocí en el cole.**
Mark	Ajá. Y ahora, **¿estudias o trabajas?**
Lola	¡Qué gracioso!
Mark	¿Gracioso? ¿Por qué?
Lola	Es la típica frase que dice un tío cuando quiere ligar.
Mark	¡Je je! Ya lo sé. Bueno, **¿a qué te dedicas?**
Lola	**Soy periodista.**
Mark	¿Ah, sí? ¿Para qué periódico escribes?
Lola	*¡Hola!*
Mark	Hola, encanto. Pero pensé que ya nos habíamos saludado.
Lola	Así se llama la revista, tonto.
Mark	¡Ah, sí! La que cuenta la vida íntima de los famosos...
Lola	Justo. La reina de la prensa rosa. Y tú, **¿qué haces?**
Mark	**Soy fotógrafo**, ¡un paparazzi!
Lola	**¡Anda ya!**
Mark	Es una broma. ¡"Estoy tirando de tu pierna"!
Lola	¿Cómo? ¡Ah! **¡Me estás tomando el pelo!**

¿ESTUDIAS O TRABAJAS?

Mark	Excuse me, **do you have a light**?
Lola	I'm sorry, I don't smoke.
Mark	Never mind. By the way, my name's Mark.
Lola	I'm Lola. **Where are you from**?
Mark	**I'm American, from Chicago.**
Lola	Oh! That explains your accent.
Mark	And **have you known Pili for long**?
Lola	**Forever.** Just imagine, **I met her in grade school.**
Mark	Ah-hah. And now, **are you studying or working**?
Lola	Very funny!
Mark	Funny? Why?
Lola	That's a typical pick-up line. [literally, *it's the typical phrase a guy says when he wants to pick someone up*]
Mark	Ha ha! I know. So, **what do you do**?
Lola	**I'm a journalist.**
Mark	Really? What newspaper do you write for?
Lola	*Hello!*
Mark	Hello, gorgeous. Though I thought we'd already said hello.
Lola	That's the name of the magazine, silly.
Mark	Oh yeah! The one that talks about the private lives of celebrities . . .
Lola	Exactly. The queen of the gossip rags [literally, *the pink press*]. **And what do you do**?
Mark	**I'm a photographer**, a paparazzi!
Lola	**Come on!**
Mark	It's a joke. I'm "pulling your leg"! [English idiom]
Lola	What? Oh! *You're taking my hair!* [Spanish equivalent of *You're pulling my leg.*]

23

Nationality

¿De dónde eres?	Where are you from?
¿Eres de (aquí/Madrid)?	Are you from (here/Madrid)?
Soy...	I'm . . .
american@ *or* de Estados Unidos	American *or* from the United States
australian@ *or* de Australia	Australian *or* from Australia
canadiense *or* de Canadá	Canadian *or* from Canada
escocés/escocesa *or* de Escocia	Scottish *or* from Scotland
galés/galesa *or* de Gales	Welsh *or* from Wales
inglés/inglesa *or* de Inglaterra	English *or* from England
irlandés/irlandesa *or* de Irlanda	Irish *or* from Ireland
neozelandés/neozelandesa *or* de Nueva Zelanda	a New Zealander *or* from New Zealand

Visit/Stay Abroad

¿Cuánto tiempo...?	How long . . . ? (*literally,* How much time . . . ?)
¿Hasta cuando...?	How long . . . ? (*literally,* Until when . . . ?)
te quedas	are you staying (for)
vas a estar aquí*	will you be here
te vas a quedar	are you going to stay (for)
Me quedo...	I'm staying . . .
Voy a estar...	I'm going to be around . . .
Me voy a quedar...	I'm going to stay . . .
unos días	several days
un par de semanas	a couple of weeks
hasta (el lunes)	until (Monday)
¿Cuánto tiempo llevas aquí*?	How long have you been here?
¿Llevas mucho tiempo aquí*?	Have you been here for a long time?
¿Desde cuándo estás aquí*?	How long have you been here?
Llevo aquí*...	I've been here . . .

---

*Use **acá** instead of **aquí** in Latin America.

Estoy aquí* desde hace...	I've been here . . .
dos días	two days
una semana	a week
tres meses	three months
Estoy de paso.	I'm just passing through.

Mutual Friends/Acquaintances

¿De qué conoces a (Pepa)?	How do you know (Pepa)?
¿Hace mucho que conoces a (Pili)?	Have you known (Pili) for long?
¿De qué os conocéis? [SP]	How do you know each other?
¿De qué se conocen? [LA]	How do you know each other?
¿Os conocéis desde hace mucho? [SP]	Have you known each other for long?
¿Se conocen desde hace mucho? [LA]	Have you known each other for long?

~~~~~~

Verb Alert! • Conocer

Remember that **conocer** can mean either *to know* or *to meet*. The meaning is usually clear from the context. Generally the verb means *to know* when it's in the present tense:

¿Conoces a Pepa?	Do you know Pepa?
La conozco desde la infancia.	I've known her since we were kids.

But it means *to meet* when it's in the past tense:

¿Dónde lo conociste?	Where did you meet him?
Lo conocí en el trabajo.	I met him at work.

Also, be careful not to confuse *conocer* with *saber*. *Conocer* means "know" in the sense of *being personally acquainted with someone or something* (a person or place, for example). *Saber* indicates *ability* (*Sabe nadar* = He knows how to swim) and *knowledge in the general sense*.

~~~~~~

¿**Hace mucho que sois amigos?** [SP]	Have you been friends for long?
¿**Hace mucho que son amigos?** [LA]	Have you been friends for long?
Conozco a (Pili)...	I've known (Pili) . . .
Nos conocemos...	We've known each other . . .
Somos amigos...	We've been friends . . .
de toda la vida	forever
desde hace mucho tiempo	for a long time
desde hace poco	for a short time
desde la infancia	since we were kids
¿**Cuándo os conocisteis?** [SP]	When did you meet?
¿**Cuándo se conocieron?** [LA]	When did you meet?

Culture Flash • The Work "Taboo"

In the opening dialogue Mark asks Lola what she does when they've just met—a totally normal icebreaker in the USA, Britain, and the English-speaking world in general. But watch out: this is *not* a question you want to pop right off with native Spanish speakers.

This is probably because in Latin cultures "who you are"—that is, your personality—is more important than "what you do," which is often considered irrelevant or of secondary importance. Also, if you ask someone what they do straight off, chances are they'll think you're trying to pigeonhole them before you've had a chance to get to know them. Our recommendation: wait until you've been chatting for a while (or even until your second encounter) before asking someone what line of work he or she is in.

As for *¿Estudias o trabajas?*, this is a classic pick-up line and so falls into a category by itself. And it flatters everyone: students by implying that they look mature enough to be out in the working world and working adults by implying that they look young enough to be students.

Nos conocimos...	We met . . .
en el trabajo	at work
en el cole☺ [SP]	in (grade) school
en un curso	in a course
en un viaje	on a trip
en una fiesta	at a party

Occupation

¿A qué te dedicas?	What do you do for a living?
¿Qué haces?	What do you do?
¿En qué trabajas?	What do you do?
¿Cuál es tu profesión?	What line of work are you in?
Soy...	I'm a . . .
enfermer@	nurse
estudiante	student
informátic@	computer analyst/ programmer
periodista	journalist
profesor/a	teacher

For more professions, see pages 181–182 in the Word Bank.

¿Qué estudias?	What are you studying?
¿Qué estudiaste?	What did you study?
¿Qué carrera has hecho?	What did you major in? What did you study in college/ at university?
Estudio...	I'm studying . . .
Estudié...	I studied . . .
Hice...	I did . . . /I majored in . . .
Soy licienciad@ en...	I have a degree in . . .
bellas artes	fine arts
derecho	law
informática	computer science
medicina	medicine
psicología	psychology

For more majors and degree programs, see pages 175–176 in the Word Bank.

Showing Surprise or Disbelief

¿Ah sí?	Really?
¡No me digas!	You don't say!
¿En serio?	Are you serious?
¡Anda ya!☻ [SP]	Come on!/I don't believe it!
¡Qué dices!☻ [SP]	Come on!
¡Estás bromeando!	You're joking!
¡Me estás tomando el pelo!☺	You're pulling my leg!
¡No fastidies!☻ [SP]	You're kidding!

Grammar Flash • It's Not *Your* Body

ME ESTÁS TOMANDO EL PELO

Note that in Spanish you usually use a definite article—**el**, **la**, **los**, **las**—*not* a possessive pronoun, before body parts. And if you're referring to a physical sensation (such as pain) or if someone else is doing something to you, tack on a personal pronoun—**me**, **te**, etc.—before the verb.

~~Abre tus ojos.~~ Abre *los* ojos.	Open your eyes.
~~Levanta tu brazo.~~ Levanta *el* brazo.	Raise your arm.
~~Mi rodilla duele.~~ *Me* duele *la* rodilla.	My knee hurts.
~~¡Estás tomando mi pelo!~~	You're pulling
¡*Me* estás tomando *el* pelo!	my leg!

Common Pick-up Lines

¿Estás acompañad@?	Are you with someone?
¿Estudias o trabajas?	Are you studying or working?
¿Me dejas que me presente?	Let me introduce myself.
Me suena (mucho) tu cara.	Your face is (really) familiar.
¿Nos conocemos?	Have we met?
No eres de aquí, ¿verdad?	You're not from around here, are you?
¿Te importa si me siento aquí?	Do you mind if I sit here?
¿Tienes fuego?	Do you have a light?

Slang Flash • ligar 😊 [SP]

This verb (which literally means *to tie* or *bind*) crops up a lot in informal conversations in Spain, and is also common in Mexico. Though it has no real English equivalent, it can be loosely translated as *to score* or *pick someone up*. But in fact **ligar** is a fabulously ambiguous catch-all word that covers anything resulting from two people meeting and feeling attracted to each other . . .

He ligado.
{ I met someone.
I flirted (with someone).
I scored.
I hooked up (with someone).
I got off (with someone).

On the Spot

A   *You're talking with someone at your friend Paco's party. Fill in the
blanks in your conversation.*

Tú   Perdón, ¿tienes (1)_____?

Él/Ella   Sí, toma. *(Person hands you a lighter.)*

Tú   Gracias.

Él/Ella   No eres de aquí, ¿verdad?

Tú   No, soy (2)_____. *[Write your nationality.]*

Él/Ella   ¿Ah, sí? ¿Y cuánto tiempo (3)_____ aquí?

Tú   Muy poco. Una semana.

Él/Ella   ¿Y de qué (4)_____ a Paco?

Tú   Es amigo de un amigo. Y tú, ¿le conoces desde
(5)_____ mucho?

Él/Ella   De (6)_____ la vida. Somos amigos
(7)_____ la infancia.

B *You're at a bar. The guy next to you is trying to pick someone up. Fill in the blanks in the conversation you overhear between them.*

Él   Perdón, ¿tienes hora?

Ella   Lo siento, no llevo reloj.

Él   No importa. Tienes acento. ¿De dónde (1) _____?

Ella   De Irlanda.

Él   ¿Ah, sí? Bonito país. Y ¿estudias o (2) _____?

Ella   Trabajo. No soy tan joven.

Él   Pues lo pareces. En fin, ¿a qué te (3) _____?

Ella   ¿Cómo?

Él   ¿Qué (4) _____?

Ella   (5) _____ profesora de inglés.

Él   ¡No me (6) _____! Estoy buscando una profesora de inglés para darme clases.

Ella   ¡Anda ya! ¡Me estás (7) _____ el pelo!

Él   No, te lo digo en serio. ¿Cuándo podemos empezar?

4

Asking for Help or Info

The following day, Mark drops by to help Pili clean up after the party.

Pili   Mark, **¿me echas una mano?**

Mark   **¿Perdona?**

Pili   **¿Me ayudas con esto, porfa?** Pesa un montón.

Mark   ¡Ah! **Sí, claro.**

(Los dos mueven una mesa a un rincón del salón.)

Pili   Gracias.

Mark   De nada. Oye, **¿tienes hora?**

Pili   Sí, son las siete y media pasadas.

Mark   **¿Cómo? ¿Me lo puedes repetir?**

Pili   Sí, un poco después de las siete y media. ¿Por qué? ¿Has quedado?

Mark   No, pero tengo que ir a una ferretería antes de que cierre. **¿Hay alguna por aquí?**

Pili   Sí, a dos manzanas, esquina con San Bernardo.

Mark   Estupendo. Es que necesito un... **¿cómo se llama ese chisme que hace agujeros en la pared?**

Pili   ¿Un taladro? Pero si yo tengo uno. Te lo dejo, si quieres.

Mark   ¿Ah, sí? **¿Me lo prestas unos días?**

Pili   **¿Cómo no?** *(Va a buscar el taladro y se lo da.)* **Toma.**

Mark   Qué bien, gracias. ¡Ah!, y otra cosa. **¿Puedo hacer una llamada?**

Pili   ¿Una llamada? **¡Ni hablar!**

Mark   **¿Cómo?**

Pili   **¡Ni se te ocurra!**

Mark   No entiendo.

Pili   Era una broma. **Claro que sí.** El teléfono está allí.

¿CÓMO SE LLAMA ESE CHISME...?

Pili	Mark, **will you give me a hand?**
Mark	**Excuse me?**
Pili	**Will you help me with this, please?** It weighs a ton.
Mark	Oh! **Yeah, sure.**

(They move a table to a corner in the living room.)

Pili	Thanks.
Mark	Sure. Hey, **do you have the time?**
Pili	Yeah, it's just after seven thirty.
Mark	**What? Can you say that again?**
Pili	Yes, a little after seven thirty. Why? Are you supposed to be some place?
Mark	No, but I have to get to a hardware store before it closes. **Is there one nearby?**
Pili	Yes, two blocks away, on the corner of San Bernardo.
Mark	Great. The thing is I need a . . . **what's that thingamajig that makes holes in the wall called?**
Pili	A drill? Hey, but I have one. I can lend it to you, if you want.
Mark	Oh yeah? **Can you lend it to me for a few days?**
Pili	**Of course.** *(She goes off to get the drill and gives it to him.)* **Here you are.**
Mark	Great, thanks. Oh, and one more thing. **Can I make a phone call?**
Pili	A phone call? **No way!**
Mark	**What?**
Pili	**Don't even think of it!**
Mark	I don't understand.
Pili	I was kidding. **Of course you can.** The telephone's over there.

When You Don't Understand

¿Cómo?	Excuse me?/What?
¿Perdón?/¿Perdona?	Excuse me?/Sorry?
¿Qué (has dicho)?	What (did you say)?
¿Qué decías?	What were you saying?
¿Puedes repetirlo?	Can you repeat that?
¿Puedes hablar más alto?	Can you speak louder?
¿Puedes hablar más despacio?	Can you speak more slowly?
¿Me lo vuelves a explicar?	Can you explain that to me again?
No te he entendido.	I didn't understand that.
No lo he captado.☺	I didn't get that.
No me he enterado.☺ [SP]	I don't get it.
No te he oído.	I didn't catch that.
No estaba prestando atención.	I wasn't paying attention.

Excusing Yourself • perdón/perdona

These both mean *excuse me*, though note that **perdona** is more informal than **perdón**, and should be limited to close friends or family. Use them in the following situations:

1. to get someone to repeat something (when you didn't hear or understand them)
2. to catch someone's attention
3. to excuse yourself for trying to get by someone when your path is blocked or when you cause a minor inconvenience (bumping into someone, stepping on a person's foot, and so on)

An alternative is **disculpa** (familiar, used with *tú*) or **disculpe** (formal, used with *Ud.*). These are a bit more formal than **perdón/perdona** and very common in Latin America.

Asking About a Word

¿Cómo se llama...?	What's . . . called?
esto	this
eso	that
esa cosa (que se usa para tostar pan)	that thing (that you use to toast bread)
ese chisme☺ [SP] (que hace agujeros en la pared)	that gadget/thingamajig/whatchamacallit (that makes holes in the wall)

¿Cómo se dice "drill"?	How do you say "drill"?
¿Cómo se escribe "taladro"?	How do you spell "taladro"?
¿Qué significa "taladro"?	What does "taladro" mean?
¿Qué quiere decir "taladro"?	What does "taladro" mean?

Making Sure That Someone Understands

¿Me entiendes?	Do you understand?
¿Lo captas?☺	Do you get it?
¿Me explico?	Is that clear?
No sé si me explico.	Do you follow me? *(more polite)*
¿Me has entendido?	Did you understand?
¿Lo has captado?☺	Did you get that?
¿Me he explicado?	Was that clear?
No sé si me he explicado bien.	Did you understand? *(more polite)*

Asking for a Favor

¿Me haces un favor?	Can you do me a favor?
¿Te puedo pedir un favor?	Can I ask you a favor?
¿Me ayudas (con esto)?	Will you help me (with this)?
¿Me echas una mano?☺	Can you give me a hand?/Can you help me out?

¿Me das...?	Can you give me . . . ?
¿Me dejas...? [SP]	Can you lend me . . . ?
¿Me prestas...?	Can you lend me . . . ?
un bolígrafo	a pen
una toalla	a towel
ese libro	that book

¿Me pasas...?	Can you pass me . . . ?
¿Me acercas...?	Can you pass me . . . ?
la sal	the salt
el azúcar	the sugar
el cenicero	the ashtray
¿Me acercas...? [SP]	Can you give me a lift . . . ?
¿Me puedes llevar...?	Can you give me a ride . . . ?
a casa	home
al hotel	to the hotel
a la estación	to the station
¿Puedes...?	Can you . . . ?
subir/bajar el volumen	turn up/turn down the volume
abrir/cerrar la ventana	open/close the window
encender/apagar la luz	turn on/turn off the light

Idiom Flash • echar una mano (a alguien) ☺

¿ME ECHAS UNA MANO?

This is the Spanish equivalent of *to give* or *lend a hand*. It means, literally, "to throw a hand" to someone.

¿Me echas una mano?	Will you give me a hand?
Mis amigos me echaron una mano.	My friends helped me out.
Le eché una mano con la mudanza.	I helped him with his move.

Asking for Permission

¿Puedo...?	Can I . . . ?
fumar	smoke
tomar un vaso de agua	have a glass of water
usar el baño	use the bathroom
¿Me dejas...?/¿Me permites...?	Will you let me . . . ?
conectarme a Internet	get on the Internet
hacer una llamada	make a phone call
llamar desde tu celular [LA]	make a call from your cell phone
llamar desde tu móvil [SP]	make a call from your cell phone

Responding
Affirmative

Claro que sí.	Of course. (*emphatic*)
¿Cómo no?	Of course.
OK.☺ [LA]	OK.
Sí, claro.	Yes, of course.
Sí, por supuesto.	Yes, of course.
Vale.☺ [SP]	OK./Sure.
Toma./Ten.	Here you are.
Aquí lo/la tienes.	Here you are.

Negative

No, lo siento.	No, I'm sorry.
Mira, lo siento, pero mejor no.	Look, I'm sorry, but I'd rather you didn't.
Va a ser que no.☺ [SP]	Uh-uh. (*literally,* it's going to be no)
¡Ni hablar!☺*	No way!
¡Ni en broma!☺ [SP]*	You must be joking!
¡Ni se te ocurra!☺*	Don't even think of it!
¡Ni soñarlo!☺*	Don't even dream of it!

---

*Very strong, but can be said affectionately and/or jokingly among *amigos*.

Culture Flash • Thanks, No Thanks

Note that none of the questions in this unit include the word **por favor**. There's a reason for this. The fact is **por favor** and **gracias** just aren't bandied about in Spanish as much as they are in English (particularly in Spain; in Latin America, people are a little more formal and polite).

As a rule of thumb, reserve **por favor** for interactions with strangers (waiters, clerks, and so on). Even then, don't overdo it, as it can seem overly polite and affected. Among *amigos,* slash this word from your repertoire, or else use it sparingly. Another option (used a lot by young people in Spain) is to say **porfa** (the slangy abbreviation of **por favor**), which has a more casual, tongue-in-cheek feel to it.

As for **gracias**, this is a *little* more common, but don't make a habit of thanking people for everything. Our recommendation: reserve that **gracias** for special favors (your pal's treated you to a lobster dinner or lent you his car) and major acts of heroism (someone's rescued you from a burning building, or saved you from financial ruin). And then let your instincts guide you: there'll always be moments when a heartfelt **gracias** hits the spot.

Asking the Time and Date

¿Qué hora es?	What time is it?
¿Tienes hora?	Do you have the time?
¿Qué día es hoy?	What day is today?
¿Qué fecha es hoy?	What's today's date?
¿A qué (fecha) estamos hoy?	What's today's date?
¿A qué día estamos?	What day is it?
¿En qué mes/año estamos?	What month/year is it?

For ways to say the time and date, see pages 177–178 in the Word Bank.

Asking When Things Are

¿Cuándo...?	When . . . ?
¿A qué hora...?	What time . . . ?
empieza la película	does the movie begin
es el concierto	is the concert
sale el tren	does the train leave
llega tu amig@	is your friend arriving
habéis [SP]/han [LA] quedado	are you meeting up
sales de clase/del trabajo	do you finish class/work

Asking for Directions

¿Cómo llego (a tu casa/ al hotel)?	How do I get (to your house/ to the hotel)?
¿Cómo hago para llegar a (tu casa)?	How do I get to (your house)?
¿Hay... cerca?	Is there . . . nearby?
¿Hay... por aquí?	Is there . . . around here?
algún banco	a bank
alguna farmacia	a drugstore
alguna ferretería	a hardware store
algún metro	a subway
algún quiosco	a newsstand

For more stores, see page 172 in the Word Bank.

For common words in giving directions, see page 163 in the Word Bank.

Basic Survival Flash • Asking Strangers for Directions

OK, here you definitely use **por favor**. But that's all . . .

¿La Plaza Mayor, por favor?	Could you tell me how to get to the Plaza Mayor, please?
¿La calle Atocha, por favor?	How do I get to Atocha Street, please?

Asking Where Things Are

¿Dónde está...?	Where is . . . ?
¿Por dónde queda...?	Whereabouts is . . . ?
tu casa	your house
el restaurante	the restaurant
el cine	the movie theater
el bar	the bar
¿A qué distancia está...?	How far is . . . ?
¿Está cerca/lejos...?	Is . . . near/far . . .?
tu casa (del metro)	your house (from the subway)
Segovia (de Madrid)	Segovia (from Madrid)

On the Spot

A *Mark and Pili continue talking. Fill in the blanks in their conversation.*

Mark Entonces, ¿cómo se (1) _____ esto? *(Señala el taladro.)*

Pili Taladro.

Mark ¡Ah, sí! Oye, ¿me (2) _____ un bolígrafo?

Pili Sí, claro. (3) _____. *(Le da el bolígrafo.)*

Mark Gracias. ¿Y cómo se (4) _____ "taladro"?

Pili T-A-L-A-D-R-O.

(Mark escribe "taladro" en el papel.)

Mark Bien. Así no se me olvida. ¡Ah!, y otra cosa. ¿Cómo se
(5) _____ "hammer" en español? *(Con la mano imita el movimiento de un martillo.)*

Pili ¡Ah! Un *martillo.*

Mark Ajá. Pues ¿te puedo (6) _____ otro favor?

Pili Dime.

Mark ¿Tienes uno?

Pili ¿Un martillo? Creo que sí.

Mark ¿Me lo (7) _____ unos días?

Pili Claro. ¿Cómo (8) _____?

B *You're talking to Pepa. Fill in the blanks in your conversation.*

Pepa   Oye, ¿qué (1) _____ es?

Tú   Las ocho y cuarto. ¿Por qué?

Pepa   Pues vamos un poco justos de tiempo.

Tú   ¿(2) _____? No te he (3) _____ .

Pepa   Que vamos a llegar tarde a la película.

Tú   ¡Ah! ¿A qué (4) _____ empieza?

Pepa   A las ocho y media.

Tú   ¿Y está (5) _____ el cine?

Pepa   No, está cerca. A diez minutos andando. Pero venga, tenemos que salir ya.

5

Likes and Dislikes

Mark and Pili are talking in a bar.

Mark   **Me gusta este grupo.**

Pili   **¿A que mola?**

Mark   **Sí, es genial. Me encanta.**

Pili   Pues esta noche actúan en la "Sala Sol". ¿Quieres venir?

Mark   Por supuesto. **¡Qué maravilla!**

Pili   Lola va a ir también. **Le apasiona el rock.**

Mark   ¿Lola?

Pili   Sí, la chica con quien estabas hablando en mi fiesta.

Mark   ¡Ah, sí! La periodista... Es **muy simpática.**

Pili   Pues **tú le caes muy bien** también.

Mark   ¿Ah, sí? Me alegro.

Pili   ¿Qué pasa? **¿Te gusta mi amiga?**

Mark   Sí, ya te lo dije. **Me parece muy simpática.**

Pili   Ya, pero, **¿te gusta? ¿Te parece atractiva?**

Mark   ¡Ah! ¿Por qué me lo preguntas?

Pili   Por curiosidad. En fin, **me da lo mismo.**

Mark   Bueno... **me gusta un poco.**

Pili   Ya me lo imaginaba.

Mark   A pesar de que es periodista...

Pili   ¿Qué tienes contra los periodistas?

Mark   **No los soporto.** Siempre te están interrogando.

Pili   Es verdad. **Son un poco** pesados.

Mark   Pero Lola no es así. **Es encantadora...**

Mark	I like this band.
Pili	Isn't it cool?
Mark	Yeah, it's great. I love it.
Pili	Well, tonight they're performing at "Sala Sol." Want to come?
Mark	Of course. Great!
Pili	Lola's going too. She's really into rock.
Mark	Lola?
Pili	Yes, the girl you were talking to at my party.
Mark	Oh yeah! The journalist . . . She's really nice.
Pili	Well, she likes you a lot too.
Mark	Oh really? I'm glad to hear that.
Pili	What's the matter? Do you like my friend? [that is, *do you find her attractive?*]
Mark	Yeah, I already told you. I think she's really nice.
Pili	I know, but do you like her? Do you find her attractive?
Mark	Oh! Why do you ask?
Pili	Just curious. Anyway, I don't care either way.
Mark	Well, I like her a little.
Pili	I figured as much.
Mark	Despite the fact that she's a journalist . . .
Pili	What do you have against journalists?
Mark	I can't take them. They're always interrogating you.
Pili	That's true. They're a bit of a pain.
Mark	But Lola's not like that. She's great . . .

Expressing Likes

Me gusta (mucho)...	I (really) like . . .
la comida mexicana	Mexican food
viajar	traveling
que me hagan regalos	being given presents
Me encanta...	I love . . .
la música brasileña	Brazilian music
bailar	dancing
que me mimen	being spoiled

Me gusta Alternatives

Me hace (mucha) gracia...☺ [SP]	I (really) like . . .
esa chaqueta	that jacket
tu perro	your dog
Me divierte (mucho)...	I (really) like/enjoy . . .
	(used for activities)
Me entretiene (mucho)...	I (really) like/enjoy . . .
	(used for activities)
la lectura	reading
oír la radio	listening to the radio
dibujar	drawing

Me encanta Alternatives

Me apasiona...	I love . . .
Me chifla...☻ [SP]	I love . . .
Me fascina...☺ [LA]	I love . . .
Me enloquece...☺	I'm crazy about . . .
Me vuelve loc@...☺	I'm nuts about . . .
el flamenco	flamenco
ese escritor/esa escritora	that writer
ese cuadro	that painting

~~~~~~

Grammar Flash • Me gusta, me encanta...

Note that when you express like (or dislike) in Spanish, the subject/object roles are reversed.

Me gusta viajar. (*literally,* traveling is appealing to me) — I like traveling.

Me encanta la música brasileña. (*literally,* Brazilian music enchants me) — I love Brazilian music.

The same goes for **me entretiene, me apasiona, me fascina, me irrita,** and all the other expressions starting with **me.** Note also that if the thing you like or dislike (that is, the thing that's appealing, enchanting, irritating, or unbearable to you) is in the plural form, the verb needs to be plural too.

Me *gustan* los gatos. — I like cats.
Me *espantan* las arañas. — I hate spiders.

~~~~~~

Expressing Dislikes

No me gusta (nada)...	I don't like . . . (at all)
ese color	that color
ir con prisas	having to rush
que me mientan	being lied to
No me hace (ninguna) gracia...☺[SP]	I don't like . . . (at all)
Me desagrada...	. . . turns me off
ese pintor/esa pintora	that painter
esperar	waiting
que me den plantón	being stood up

Me espanta...	I hate . . .
Me horroriza...	I hate . . .
ese cuadro	that painting
madrugar	getting up early
No soporto...	I can't bear . . .
No aguanto...	I can't take/stand . . .
a los niños mimados	spoiled children
que me timen	being conned/cheated
Me saca de quicio...☺	. . . drives me up the wall.
Me irrita...	. . . irritates me.
Me revienta...	. . . riles me.
Me pone enferm@...☺ [SP]	. . . makes me sick.
Me enferma...☺ [LA]	. . . makes me sick.
Me toca las narices...☻ [SP]	. . . really gets my goat.
ese tío [SP]/ese tipo [LA]	that guy
que me estafen	being ripped off/swindled
Detesto...	I hate . . . (*very strong*)
Odio...	I hate . . . (*very strong*)
a los dictadores	dictators
madrugar	getting up early

Exclamations

¡Cuánto me gusta (este vino)!	I just love (this wine)!
¡Qué maravilla!	Wow! (That's/It's) great/fantastic/amazing!
¡Qué horror!	How awful!/That's terrible! (*very common*)
¡Qué espanto!	That's awful! (*stronger version of* ¡Qué horror!*)

Other Expressions

Soy muy aficionad@ (al jazz).	I'm really into (jazz).
Soy un/a forof@☺ [SP] (del jazz).	I'm a (jazz) nut.
Mola.☻ [SP]	It rules./It's really cool.
Es guai.☻ [SP]	It's cool. (*pronounced "why"*)
Es la bomba.☻	It's awesome.
Es lo máximo.☻ [LA]	It's the best.

~~~~~~

Culture Flash • Latin Passion

You've heard about Latin passion? Well, now's the time to apply it. When it comes to expressing your feelings about things in Spanish, forget about sitting on the fence or making noncommittal or lukewarm declarations. Particularly in conversational Spanish, the tendency is to be as vocal and dramatic as possible. So go with your gut feeling, and let all rip. Do you like Mexican food? Say it with a little passion. **¡Me encanta! ¡Qué maravilla!** Do you dislike waiting on line? Don't mince your words. **¡Me horroriza! ¡Qué espanto!** Get the picture? And, once you get into it, you'll find a little melodrama is fun . . .

~~~~~~

¿A que mola? [SP]	Isn't it cool?/Don't you think it's cool?
¿A que es guai? [SP]	Isn't it cool?/Don't you think it's cool?
¿A que es la bomba?	Isn't it awesome?/Don't you think it's awesome?
No me dice nada.	It doesn't do anything for me.
Me trae sin cuidado.	It leaves me cold.
Ni me va ni me viene.	It doesn't do anything for me.
Paso de... [SP]	I have no interest in . . . /I'm not into . . .
los sitios turísticos	touristy places
ver una película doblada	seeing a dubbed movie

Verb Alert! • gustar

Watch out! If you use **gustar** in reference to people, it has sexual/romantic connotations.

Me gusta tu hermano.	I like your brother. (that is, *I think he's cute* or *attractive*)

If you like someone's brother, but not *that way*, use **caer bien**.

Me cae bien tu hermano.	I like your brother. (that is, *I think he's nice*)

Gustar doesn't have sexual/romantic connotations, though, if you're talking about a public personality or someone you don't know personally—an actor or writer, for example.

Me gusta esa escritora.	I like that writer. (that is, *the way she writes*)

Expressing a Liking for People

Me cae (muy) bien (Pili).	I (really) like (Pili).
Aprecio (mucho) a (Pili).	I (really) value/appreciate (Pili).
Adoro a (Pili).	I adore (Pili).
Me encanta (Pili).	I love (Pili).
Me gusta (Pili).	I like (Pili). (*has sexual/romantic connotations*)
(Luis/Pepa) es...	(Luis/Pepa) is . . .
encantador/a	great (*literally,* charming)
muy simpátic@	really nice
un encanto	great (*literally,* a charm)
muy gracios@	really funny
muy maj@☺ [SP]	really nice
muy salad@	really amusing/lively

Key Words • *encanto* and *encantador/a*

Yes, *charm* and *charming* sound a little quaint and affected in English. But in Spanish, **encanto** and **encantador/a** are pretty standard fare. So forget the literal translation, and use these words when you want to say a person, place, or thing is really great or special.

Tu hermano es encantador.	Your brother is really great.
Es un sitio con encanto.	It's a really special place.
Es una mujer encantadora.	She's a wonderful woman.
Luis tiene mucho encanto.	Luis is totally adorable.

Expressing Dislike for People

Me cae mal (Pepa).	I don't like (Pepa).
No me cae bien (Pepa).	I don't like (Pepa).
Le tengo manía a (Pepa).☺ [SP]	(Pepa) rubs me the wrong way.
No conecto con (Pepa).	I don't really connect with (Pepa).
No me llevo bien con (Pepa).	I don't really get on with (Pepa).
(Luis/Pepa) es muy/un poco...	(Luis/Pepa) is very/a little/a bit of . . .
antipátic@	unfriendly
rar@	weird
pesad@	boring/a pain
petard@☻ [SP]	a dud/a bore

Stating a Preference

Prefiero...	I prefer . . .
(Segovia) a/que (Toledo)	(Segovia) to (Toledo)
(la comida japonesa) a/que (la china)	(Japanese) to (Chinese food)
(leer) a/que (ver la tele)	(reading) to (watching TV)

Me gusta más...	I like . . . better . . .
(París) que (Roma)	(Paris) than (Rome)
(el monte) que (la playa)	(the mountains) than (the beach)
(dar) que (recibir)	(giving) than (receiving)
De todos los deportes...	Of all sports . . .
me quedo con (el tenis)	I like (tennis) best
(el fútbol) es mi favorito	(soccer) is my favorite
(el baloncesto) es mi preferido	(basketball) is my favorite

Or Lack of Preference/Indifference

No tengo preferencias.	I don't have a preference.
Me es indiferente.	I don't care either way.
Me es igual.	It's the same to me.
Me es lo mismo.	It's the same to me.
Me da igual.	It's the same to me.
Me da lo mismo.	It's the same to me.

On the Spot

A   *Pili and Lola are having a little girl talk. Fill in the blanks in their conversation.*

Pili   Oye, Lola, ¿sabes que tú le (1)_____ a Mark?

Lola   ¿Ah, sí?

Pili   Eso me dijo. En fin, ¿a ti te (2)_____?

Lola   No sé. Me cae (3)_____. Aunque es un poco pesado.

Pili   ¿Pesado? ¿Por qué?

Lola   No paraba de interrogarme. Una pregunta tras otra...

Pili   ¡Qué horror!

Lola   Sí, no me hace mucha (4)_____ cuando te interrogan así.

Pili   Entonces ¡te (5)_____ fatal!

Lola   No, porque es gracioso. Después me reí mucho con él.

Pili   Y ¿no te (6)_____ atractivo?

Lola   No sé. No está mal...

B   *You and Pili are at a music bar. Fill in the gaps in your conversation.*

Pili   ¿Te (1) _____ este grupo que está tocando?

Tú   No sé. En fin, no me (2) _____ nada.

Pili   ¿Ah, no? A mí me (3) _____. Es uno de mis grupos preferidos.

Tú   ¿Y el que estaba tocando antes?

Pili   ¡Ah, no! ¡Qué (4) _____! No me gusta
(5) _____.

Tú   A mí sí. Y el cantante me vuelve (6) _____.

6

Wishing and Wanting

Pepa, Pili, and Mark meet up the day after the concert.

Pepa	¿Qué tal el concierto anoche?
Mark	Buenísimo.
Pili	Sí, **te hubiera encantado**.
Pepa	Ya, **me lo perdí**. **Me quedé con las ganas**.
Pili	Pues nada, **otra vez será**.
Pepa	**Eso espero**. Oye, por cierto, ¿qué vas a hacer este fin de semana?
Pili	No sé. ¿Por qué?
Pepa	¡Es que **tengo unas ganas de salir de Madrid**...! ¿Por qué no hacemos una excursión?
Mark	No es mala idea.
Pili	Sí, **a mí también me apetece una escapada**.
Pepa	Estupendo. ¿Qué os parece Segovia?
Pili	**Yo por mí, encantada**. Fui hace años, y **estoy deseando volver**.
Pepa	¿Y tú, Mark?
Mark	**Me gustaría conocerlo**. Nunca he estado.
Pepa	Pues ya está. ¿Vamos el sábado?
Pili	Vale. Y a ver si **quiere venir** Lola también.
Mark	¿Lola? ¡Ah, sí! **¡Ojalá!**
Pili	Oye, y ya que vamos, **no me importaría tomar un buen cochinillo**.
Mark	¿Qué es eso?
Pepa	Un plato típico de Segovia. Un cerdito recién nacido asado.
Mark	¡Qué asco! **Paso...**
Pili	**Pues tú te lo pierdes**. Está buenísimo. **¡Ay, qué ilusión!**

¡ OJALÁ !

Pepa	How was the concert last night?
Mark	Really good.
Pili	Yeah, **you'd have loved it**.
Pepa	I know, **I missed out on it. I would have liked to have gone.**
Pili	Oh well, **another time**.
Pepa	**I hope so.** Hey, by the way, what are you doing this weekend?
Pili	I don't know. Why?
Pepa	It's just that **I really feel like getting out of Madrid**! Why don't we take a day trip?
Mark	It's not a bad idea.
Pili	Yeah, **I'd like a little escape too**.
Pepa	Great. What about Segovia?
Pili	**Fine by me.** I went years ago, and **I'm dying to go back**.
Pepa	What about you, Mark?
Mark	**I'd like to go.** I've never been.
Pepa	Settled. Shall we go on Saturday?
Pili	OK. And let's see if Lola **wants to come** too.
Mark	Lola? Oh, yeah! **That'd be great!**
Pili	Hey, and now that we're going, **I wouldn't mind having a good "cochinillo"**!
Mark	What's that?
Pepa	A typical dish of Segovia. A roasted newborn little pig.
Mark	Gross! **I think I'll pass on that** . . .
Pili	Well, **it's your loss**. It's really delicious. Oh, **I can't wait**!

Expressing Desire or Enthusiasm

Quiero...	I want (to) . . .
Me gustaría...	I'd like (to) . . .
Me apetece... [SP]	I feel like . . . /I'd be into . . .
Me provoca... ☺ [LA]	I feel like . . . /I'd be into . . .
Tengo ganas de...	I feel like . . . /I really want to . . .
No me importaría (nada)...	I wouldn't mind (at all) . . .
Me molaría...☻ [SP]	I'd be into . . .
hacer una excursión	take/taking a day trip
ir al cine	go/going to the movies

Strong/Emphatic

Me encantaría...	I'd love to . . .
Me apetece mucho... [SP]	I really feel like . . . /I'd really be into . . .
Me provoca mucho...☺ [LA]	I really feel like . . . /I'd really be into . . .
Tengo muchas ganas de...	I'd love to . . . /I'd really be into . . .
Estoy deseando...	I'm dying to . . .
Me haría mucha ilusión... [SP]	I'd really like to . . .
ir a (la India)	go/going to (India)
tomar (un cochinillo)	have/having (a roast suckling pig)
Sería estupendo.	That'd be great./I'd love that.
Sería genial.☻	That'd be great./I'd love that.
Yo por mí, encantad@.	Fine by me./Great as far as I'm concerned.

Expressing Disinterest or Reluctance

No quiero...	I don't want to . . .
No me apetece... [SP]	I don't feel like . . . /I'm not in the mood to . . .
No me provoca...☺ [LA]	I don't feel like . . . /I'm not in the mood to . . .
No tengo ganas de...	I don't want to . . . /I don't feel like . . .
salir esta noche	go/going out tonight
ver esa película	see/seeing that movie

Key Phrase · *Tener ganas de* + infinitive

This is a very common expression which means *to feel eager* or *inclined* to do something—that is, *to really want to* or *really feel like* doing something.

Tengo ganas de ir al cine.	I really feel like going to the movies.
Tengo ganas de terminar este trabajo.	I really want to finish up this job.
Tengo muchas ganas de verte.	I'm really looking forward to seeing you.
¡Tengo unas ganas de salir de Madrid...!	I'm dying to get out of Madrid!
¡Qué ganas tengo de acabar esto!	I'm dying to get this over with!

Meanwhile, if you do something with *ganas*, it means you do it with *enthusiasm* or *energy*.

¡Hazlo con ganas!	Do it with enthusiasm!
¡Dilo con ganas!	Say it like you mean it!

Finally, you can *stay* or *be left with ganas*, meaning you didn't or couldn't do something you would have liked to.

Me quedé con las ganas.	I missed out on it./I would have liked to.

Strong/Emphatic

No me apetece nada... [SP]	I really don't feel like. . .
No me provoca nada... ☺ [LA]	I really don't feel like. . .
No tengo ningunas ganas de...	I have no desire to . . .
No tengo ningún interés en...	I really don't want to . . . /I have no interest in . . .
Paso de... 😈 [SP]	I have no interest in . . . /I'll pass on . . .
ir a la exposición	go/going to the exhibition
salir a cenar	go/going out for dinner

No tengo el cuerpo para...	I'm really not up for . . .
No me siento con fuerzas para...	I'm really not up for . . .
salir esta noche	going out tonight
ir al gimnasio	going to the gym
No estoy para nada.	I'm not up for anything.
No cuentes conmigo.	Count me out.
Paso.☺ [SP]	I think I'll pass on that.

Related Expressions

¡Qué ilusión! [SP]	It's so exciting! I can't wait!
¡Qué bien!	Great!
¡Estupendo!	Great!
¡Cuánto me gustaría...!	I'd love to . . . !
¡Qué ganas tengo de...!	I'm dying to . . . !
¡Tengo unas ganas locas de...!☺	I'm dying to . . . !
tomar unas vacaciones	take a vacation
salir de la ciudad	get out of the city
¡Qué pocas ganas tengo de...!	I really don't feel like . . . !
¡Qué poco me apetece...! [SP]	I really don't feel like . . . !
marcharme ahora	leaving now
trabajar	working

Expressing a Hope or Wish

Espero que...	I hope that . . .
vengas	you come
haga buen tiempo	the weather'll be good
Ojalá...	I wish . . . /If only . . .
llueva	it would rain
fuera así	that were the case
Con (un poco de) suerte...	With (a little) luck . . .
Si hay suerte...	If we're lucky . . .
quedarán entradas [SP]	there'll still be tickets
quedarán boletos [LA]	there'll still be tickets

False Friend Alert!

¡ QUÉ ILUSIÓN !

Don't be under the illusion that **una ilusión** is a false perception, mirage, or hallucinatory state. Though it can mean this, the word (which is particularly popular in Spain) almost always indicates *excitement, enthusiasm,* or *delight.* The same goes for the adjective, **ilusionad@** (also common in Latin America), which means *thrilled* or *very happy* (about something).

¡Qué ilusión verte! [SP]	It's so great to see you!
¡Me hace mucha ilusión! [SP]	I can't wait!/I'm really looking forward to it!
Está ilusionado con su nueva casa.	He's all excited about his new house.

A ver si...	I hope . . . /Let's hope . . .
hace buen tiempo	the weather's good
viene (Lola)	(Lola) comes
¡Ojalá!	I wish!/If only!
Espero que sí.	I hope so.
Esperemos que sí.	Let's hope so.
Eso espero.	I hope so.
Toca madera.	Knock on wood.

Expressing a Negative Hope or Wish

Espero que...	I hope . . .
no llueva	it doesn't rain
no gane las elecciones	he doesn't win the elections
no caiga más el dólar	the dollar doesn't fall any more
Ojalá...	Let's hope . . . /Let's keep our fingers crossed . . .
no llueva	it doesn't rain
no haya un atasco	there isn't a traffic jam
no pase	it doesn't happen
Espero que no.	I hope not.
Esperemos que no.	Let's hope not.
No me haría ninguna gracia.☺ [SP]	That really wouldn't be funny.
Sería horrible.	That would be horrible.
Sería mala suerte.	That would be bad luck.
Sería una putada.☺ [SP]	That'd be a real bummer./ That'd really suck.

Expressing Regret

Es una pena.	It's a pity.
¡Qué pena!	What a pity!
Es una lástima.	It's a shame.
¡Qué lastima!	What a shame!
Es una pena que...	It's a pity that . . .
¡Qué pena que...!	What a pity that . . . !
Es una lástima que...	It's a shame that . . .
¡Qué lástima que...!	What a shame that . . . !
no puedes venir	you can't come
no vas a estar	you won't be there
no estuviste	you weren't there
Te hubiera gustado/ encantado.	You would have liked/ loved it.
Te hubiera gustado...	You would have liked . . .
Te hubiera encantado...	You would have loved . . .
el concierto	the concert
la película	the movie
el sitio	the place

Tenías que haber venido.	You should have come.
Te echamos de menos.	We missed you.
Te lo perdiste.	You missed out on it.
Me dio pena perdérmelo/la.	I'm sorry to have missed it.
Tenía que haber ido.	I should have gone.
Me hubiera gustado.	I would have liked to.
Me hubiera gustado...	I would have liked . . .
Me dio pena no...	I was sorry not . . .
ir	to go
estar	to be there
Me lo/la perdí.	I missed out on it.
Me quedé con las ganas.	I missed out on it./I would have liked to.
Otra vez será.	Oh well, another time.

Missing (Out) • *Perder(se)* vs. *Echar de menos*

Be careful how you translate *miss*. When you're talking about a feeling, use **echar de menos** (though note that in Latin America, **extrañar** is also common). When you're talking about not making it in time to catch a bus, train, or plane, use **perder**. And when you're talking about missing out on an event (a party or concert, for example), use **perderse** (the reflexive form).

Echo de menos a mi hermano.	I miss my brother.
Te vamos a extrañar. [LA]	We're going to miss you.
Perdí el tren.	I missed the train.
Me perdí el concierto.	I missed out on the concert.

Finally, there's the informal saying *(tú) te lo pierdes* ☺, meaning *it's your loss* (that is, you're missing out or going to miss out on something).

On the Spot

A *Pili and Mark continue talking after Pepa has left. Fill in the blanks in their conversation.*

Pili   Oye, Mark, ¿se lo decimos a Lola también?

Mark   ¿Qué?

Pili   Si quiere venir a Segovia con nosotros el sábado.

Mark   ¡Ah, sí! Yo por mi, (1)_____.

Pili   Seguro que le (2)_____.

Mark   Espero que (3)_____.

Pili   Sí, Lola siempre está (4)_____ salir de excursión.

Mark   Yo también. Además, tengo (5)_____ de conocer Segovia. Dicen que es muy bonita.

Pili   Es preciosa, ya verás.

Mark   Pero (6)_____ de tomar el cochinillo. Comer un cerdito recién nacido no me apetece (7)_____.

B *You're speaking with a friend. Fill in the blanks in your conversation.*

Tú ¿Qué tal anoche? ¿Salisteis al final?

Amiga Sí, estuvo genial. (1) _____ que haber venido.

Tú ¿Y la película?

Amiga Buenísima. Te (2) _____ encantado.

Tú Sí, tengo (3) _____ de verla.

Amiga Pues si piensas ir, llámame. No me (4) _____ verla otra vez.

Tú Vale. ¿Y luego fuisteis a la fiesta de Paco?

Amiga Claro. Estuvo muy divertido. En fin, te lo (5) _____ .

Tú Ya, me (6) _____ con las ganas.

7

Offering Help and Advice

Pepa and Mark chat as they walk along the street.

Mark	¿Te ayudo con esa bolsa?
Pepa	No, estoy bien. Me puedo apañar.
Mark	¿Seguro?
Pepa	Bueno, si insistes... Gracias, Mark, eres un cielo.
Mark	Por cierto, ¿a qué hora salimos mañana para Segovia?
Pepa	Pues yo, por mí, saldría temprano. Sobre las nueve o así.
Mark	Me parece bien. ¿Quiénes vamos al final?
Pepa	Pili, tú y yo. Lola no puede.
Mark	¿Por qué no?
Pepa	No lo sé. Estaba un poco rara cuando hablé con ella.
Mark	Es que tuvimos un malentendido el otro día, y está enfadada conmigo.
Pepa	¿Ah, sí? Pues esas cosas se resuelven hablando. ¿Por qué no la llamas?
Mark	No sé... Me da corte...
Pepa	En serio, yo que tú, la llamaría.
Mark	No lo tengo muy claro. No creo que esté muy receptiva.
Pepa	Anda, no lo pienses más. Hazme caso, y llámala.
Mark	Vale, vale. Seguiré tu consejo.

(Entran en un café y se sientan en una mesa.)

Pepa	Bueno, ¿qué vas a pedir?
Mark	No sé. ¿Qué me recomiendas?
Pepa	¿Te gusta el queso?
Mark	Mucho.
Pepa	Pues entonces pide el queso de cabra a la plancha. Está buenísimo.

NO LO PIENSES MÁS...

Mark	Can I help you with that bag?
Pepa	No, I'm OK. I can manage.
Mark	Are you sure?
Pepa	Well, if you insist . . . Thanks, Mark, you're an angel.
Mark	By the way, what time are we leaving tomorrow for Segovia?
Pepa	Well, I'm for leaving early. Around nine or so.
Mark	Sounds good. Who's finally coming?
Pepa	Pili, you, and me. Lola can't.
Mark	Why not?
Pepa	I don't know. She was acting a little strange when I talked to her.
Mark	The thing is we had a misunderstanding the other day, and she's angry at me.
Pepa	Oh yeah? Well, you need to talk it over with her. Why don't you call her?
Mark	I don't know . . . I feel weird about it.
Pepa	Seriously, if I were you, I'd call her.
Mark	I'm not so sure. I don't think she'll be very receptive.
Pepa	Come on, don't give it a second thought. Take my advice, and call her.
Mark	OK, OK. I'll do it.

(They walk into a café and sit down at a table.)

Pepa	Well, what are you going to order?
Mark	I don't know. What do you recommend?
Pepa	Do you like cheese?
Mark	A lot.
Pepa	Then order the grilled goat cheese. It's really good.

Offering Help

¿Te ayudo?	Can I help you?
¿Necesitas ayuda?	Do you need help?
¿Quieres que te ayude?	Do you want me to help you?
¿Te echo una mano?☺	Can I give you a hand?
¿Te acerco...? [SP]	Can I give you a lift . . . ?
¿Quieres que te lleve...?	Do you want a ride . . . ?
al aeropuerto	to the airport
a casa	home
a la estación	to the station
al hotel	to the hotel
¿Necesitas algo?	Do you need anything?
¿Te hace falta algo?	Do you need anything?
Dime...	Tell me . . .
Llámame...	Call me . . .
No dudes en llamarme...	Don't hesitate to call me . . .
No te cortes en	Don't be shy about calling
llamarme...☻[SP]	me . . .
si necesitas algo	if you need anything
Que sepas que puedes contar	I want you to know you can
conmigo.	count on me.

Accepting Help

Gracias por...	Thanks for . . .
acercarme [SP]	giving me a lift/ride
acompañarme	accompanying me
ayudarme (con esto)	helping me (with this)
Eres un cielo.☺	You're an angel/sweetheart/doll.
Te lo agradezco.	Thank you.
Te lo agradecería.	I'd really appreciate it./That'd be great.
Bueno, si insistes...	OK, if you insist . . .
¿No te importa?	You don't mind?
¡No sabes el favor que me	You don't know what a help
haces!	you are!

Un millón de gracias.	Thanks a million.
Ha sido una gran ayuda.	That was a big help.
Me has sacado de un apuro.	You've helped me out of a tight spot.
Ya te devolveré el favor.	I'll return the favor some day.

Refusing Help

No, estoy bien.	No, I'm OK.
No hace falta, gracias.	No, thanks, it's OK.
Gracias, lo puedo hacer yo sol@.	Thanks, I can do it/manage on my own.
Me puedo apañar.☺ [SP]	I can manage./I can get by.
No hace falta que...	You don't need to . . .
No necesito que...	I don't need you to . . .
me acompañes	accompany me
me lleves	give me a ride
me recojas	pick me up

Asking for Advice

¿Qué me recomiendas?	What do you recommend?
¿Dónde me recomiendas ir?	Where do you suggest I go?
¿Me puedes recomendar un hostal?	Can you recommend a hostel?
¿Me puedes decir un restaurante que esté bien?	Can you recommend a good restaurant?
No me decido.	I can't make up my mind.
No sé qué pedir.	I don't know what to order.
Estoy dudando entre (la sopa) y (la ensalada).	I can't make up my mind between (the soup) and (the salad).
¿Me puedes dar algún consejo?	Can you give me some advice?
¿Qué me aconsejas?	What do you advise?
¿Tú que harías (en mi lugar)?	What would you do (in my situation)?

Key Verb • recomendar

Note that **recomendar** is usually accompanied by the indirect object pronoun: **me, te, le, nos, os,** or **les**.

¿Qué *me* recomiendas?	What do you recommend (to me)?
Te recomiendo el vino de la casa.	I recommend the house wine (to you).
¿*Me* puedes recomendar un hotel?	Can you recommend a hotel (to me)?

Recommending Places, Dishes, etc.

Te recomiendo...	I recommend . . .
Ve a...	Go to . . .
ese hotel	that hotel
ese restaurante	that restaurant
Tienes que...	You have to . . .
ir a (Toledo)	go to (Toledo)
probar (el pulpo)	try (the octopus)
No te vayas sin...	Don't leave without . . .
visitar el museo	visiting the museum
ir al castillo	going to the castle

Giving Personal Advice

Te aconsejo que...	I advise you . . .
lo hagas cuanto antes	to do it as soon as possible
no lo dejes	not to put it off
¿Por qué no...?	Why don't you . . . ?
vas al médico	go to a doctor
te sinceras con él/ella	tell him/her how you feel
Si fuera/fuese tú,...	If I were you, . . .
Yo, en tu lugar,...	If I were you, . . .

Yo que tú,...	If I were you, . . .
iría	I'd go
no lo dudaría	I'd do it/I wouldn't hesitate
Hazme caso, y...	Take my advice, and . . .
llámalo	call him
vete	go
Deberías...	You should . . .
Tendrías que...	You should . . .
dejar de fumar	quit smoking
cuidarte más	take better care of yourself
No deberías...	You shouldn't . . .
No tendrías que...	You shouldn't . . .
acostarte tan tarde	go to bed so late
tomarte las cosas tan a pecho	take things so much to heart

Grammar Flash • The Conditional

As in English, one way of giving advice is using the conditional form.

Si fuera tú, no lo *dudaría*.	If I were you, I'd go ahead and do it.
Yo que tú, lo *haría* cuanto antes.	If I were you, I'd do it as soon as possible.

If you like, you can omit the *if I were you* part. In this case, start the sentence with **yo**.

Yo **no lo dudaría.**	I'd go ahead and do it.
Yo **lo haría cuanto antes.**	I'd do it as soon as possible.

You can also use the conditional to say you're in favor of doing something. In this case, insert **por mí** between the subject and verb.

Yo *por mí*, saldría temprano.	I'm for leaving early.
Yo *por mí*, iría a otro sitio.	I'm for going somewhere else.

Responding

Te voy a hacer caso.	I'm going to take your advice.
Voy a seguir tu consejo/ recomendación.	I'm going to follow your advice.
Tienes razón.	You're right.
Puede que tengas razón.	You might be right.
Está bien,	Alright,
OK,😊... [LA]	OK, . . .
Vale,😊... [SP]	OK, . . .
iré	I'll go
lo haré	I'll do it
No sé.	I don't know.
Me da corte.😊 [SP]	I feel embarrassed/shy/awkward about it.
No lo tengo tan claro.	I'm not so sure./I'm not convinced about that.
¿Crees que servirá de algo?	Do you think that'd help?
No sé si eso sería lo mejor.	I'm not sure that it'd be the best thing to do.

Pepa and Pili's Golden Tips

TOMÁTELO CON FILOSOFÍA

Here's some advice that could come in handy. Note that it's all in the imperative form here (though you can also use the conditional).

Cuídate (mucho).	Take (good) care of yourself.
Mímate (un poco). [SP]	Spoil yourself (a little).
Sé optimista.	Be optimistic.
Intenta ver el lado positivo.	Try and look on the bright side.

No te precipites.	Don't rush into anything.
Piénsatelo bien.	Think it over.
Sé prudente.	Be sensible./Don't rush into anything.
No te agobies. [SP]	Don't get stressed out about it.
No dejes que te amargue la vida. [SP]	Don't let it get to you.
Tómatelo con calma.	Don't get worked up.
Tómatelo con filosofía.	Don't let it get to you./Try and put things into perspective.
¡Espabílate!☺ [SP]	Get on the ball!
Hazlo cuanto antes.	Do it as soon as possible.
No lo dejes/pospongas.	Don't put it off.
¡Ponte las pilas!☺	Get cracking/going!/Get on it!
Intenta resolverlo.	Try and work it out.
Pasa de él/ella.☻ [SP]	Blow him/her off./Forget about him/her.
No le hagas caso.	Don't pay attention to him/her.
No le des importancia.	Don't dwell on it./Don't give it another thought.
No te comas el coco.☻ [SP]	Don't dwell on it./Don't lose any sleep over it.
Lánzate.☺ [SP]	Go for it.
¡A por él/ella/ello!	Go for him/her/it!
No lo pienses más.	Don't give it a second thought./Do it.
No le des más vueltas.	Don't give it a second thought./Just do it.
No te vas a arrepentir.	You won't regret it.

On the Spot

A   *You ask Pepa for advice on your upcoming trip to Cádiz. Fill in the blanks in your conversation.*

Tú   ¿Conoces Cádiz?

Pepa   Sí, es una ciudad maravillosa. ¿Por qué?

Tú   Voy a ir allí a pasar unos días.

Pepa   ¿Ah, sí? ¡Qué bien!

Tú   Pero no sé si alquilar un coche o ir en tren. ¿Qué (1)_____ recomiendas?

Pepa   Yo (2)_____ en tren. Es más rápido y cómodo.

Tú   ¿Y me (3)_____ decir un hotel que esté bien?

Pepa   ¡Ah, sí! Vete al Hotel de Francia. Está muy bien situado, en una plaza muy bonita en la parte antigua.

Tú   ¡Ah!, pues voy a seguir tu (4)_____.

Pepa   Pero, yo que (5)_____, reservaría cuanto antes. Muchas veces está completo.

Tú   Está (6)_____. Les llamaré hoy.

B   *You ask your friend Tom for advice. Fill in the blanks in your conversation.*

Tú   No sé (1)_____ hacer. No avanzo con el español.

Tom   ¿Por qué (2)_____ haces un curso?

Tú   Ya he hecho muchos cursos. Lo que quiero ahora es aprender expresiones y frases cotidianas, no de libro de texto.

Tom   ¡Ah! Conozco a dos chicas ideales para eso. Si (3)_____ tú, lo intentaría con ellas.

Tú   ¿Son profesoras?

Tom   No exactamente. Son personajes. En serio, (4)_____ las recomiendo.

Tú   ¿Son personajes? ¿Y cómo se llaman?

Tom   Pepa y Pili.

Tú   ¡Pepa y Pili! ¡Estás bromeando!

Tom   Escucha, hazme (5)_____, y busca un libro que se titula *Spanish Among Amigos*. Ya las conocerás. Y no te vas a (6)_____.

8

Speaking Your Mind

Mark and Lola go to an art gallery.

Lola	Oye, Mark, ¿ves ese cuadro?
Mark	Sí. ¿Por qué?
Lola	**¿Qué opinas de él?**
Mark	¿Cómo?
Lola	**¿Qué piensas de él? ¿Te gusta?**
Mark	No sé. Es original.
Lola	**¿Original?**
Mark	Sí. **¿No lo ves así?**
Lola	**¡Para nada! Me parece horroroso.**
Mark	**Me da que** no te gusta el arte contemporáneo.
Lola	**¡Qué va!** Sí que me gusta. Pero ese cuadro **me resulta muy desagradable.**
Mark	Y esa escultura, **¿qué te parece?**
Lola	**Ni fu ni fa.**
Mark	¿No te gusta? Yo lo veo genial.
Lola	Pues mira, **he cambiado de idea.** Ahora que lo dices, tiene algo.
Mark	¡Ah! Por cierto, **¿qué te pareció** la película anoche?
Lola	**Buenísima. Para mí,** es una obra maestra.
Mark	**Estoy contigo.** A mí también me gustó mucho.
Lola	**No me extrañaría nada que** ganara un Oscar.
Mark	**No creo.** Con el tema que trata...
Lola	**Te equivocas.** La eutanasia está muy de moda.
Mark	**¡Qué dices!** Es un tema muy controvertido.
Lola	**Desde luego.** Pero va ganando aceptación.
Mark	No sé yo...

Lola	Hey, Mark, do you see that painting?
Mark	Yeah. Why?
Lola	**What do you think of it?**
Mark	Excuse me?
Lola	**What do you think of it? Do you like it?**
Mark	I don't know. It's original.
Lola	**Original?**
Mark	Yes. **Don't you think so?**
Lola	**Not at all! I think it's awful.**
Mark	**I have a feeling** you don't like contemporary art.
Lola	No way! I do like it. But **I find** that painting **really unpleasant**.
Mark	**And what do you think of** that sculpture?
Lola	**I could take it or leave it.**
Mark	**Don't you like it? I think it's great.**
Lola	Well, listen, **I've changed my mind.** Now that you mention it, it's got something.
Mark	Oh, by the way, **what did you think of** the movie last night?
Lola	**Great. In my opinion,** it's a real masterpiece.
Mark	**I'm with you on that.** I liked it a lot too.
Lola	**I wouldn't be surprised if** it won an Oscar.
Mark	**I'm not so sure.** With that topic. . .
Lola	**You're wrong.** Euthanasia's really big right now.
Mark	**What are you saying?** It's a really controversial topic.
Lola	**No doubt about that.** But it's gaining acceptance.
Mark	**I'm not so sure about that** . . .

Asking for Somebody's Opinion

¿Qué te parece?	What do you think (of it)?
¿Te gusta?	Do you like it?
¿Qué opinas de (él/ella)?	What do you think of (him/her/it)?
¿Qué piensas de (él/ella)?	What do you think of (him/her/it)?
¿Cuál es tu opinión?	What's your opinion?
¿Tú qué piensas?	What do *you* think?
¿Tú cómo lo ves?	How do *you* see it?
¿Tú qué opinas?	What do *you* think?
¿Opinas como yo?	Do you feel the same way?
¿No estás de acuerdo?	Don't you agree?
¿No lo ves así?	Don't you think so?
¿No te parece?	Don't you think so?

Giving Your Opinion

Es...	It's . . .
Era...	It was . . .
Me parece...	I think it's . . .
Me pareció...	I thought it was . . .

Positive

admirable	admirable
curios@	interesting, different
divertid@	fun
divin@☺ [LA]	wonderful
estupend@	great
fabulos@	fabulous
fantástic@	fantastic
fascinante	fascinating
gracios@	funny, amusing *or* attractive, cute
impresionante	impressive
increíble	incredible

Negative

aburrid@	boring
asqueros@ [SP]	disgusting
cursi☺	corny, prissy
anodin@	bland, insipid
cutre☻ [SP]	cheap, tacky, shabby
de mal gusto	tasteless
espantos@	awful
fuerte☻	hard to take/ a bit much
horrible	horrible, awful
horroros@	awful, hideous
hortera☺ [SP]	tacky, tasteless

interesante	interesting	**insoportable**	unbearable
magníffic@	great, magnificent	**ni fu ni fa☺**	so-so, nothing to write home about
maravillos@	wonderful		
original	original	**pesad@**	boring
		repugnante	horrible, disgusting
		terroríffic@	horrific

Key Phrases • *Me parece* and *Me resulta*

Me parece...

This is by far the most common lead-in for expressing your opinion in Spanish and can be used with a limitless number of adjectives.

Me parece maravilloso.	I think it's great.
No me parece correcto.	I don't think it's right.

Me resulta...

This is the equivalent of *I find* something or someone (attractive, boring, etc.) It's generally used with adjectives that convey pleasure or displeasure, attraction or repulsion, comfort or discomfort, interest or boredom.*

Me resulta muy agradable su compañía.	I really enjoy her company. (*literally*, I find her company very pleasant)
Me resulta ofensivo.	I find it offensive.

---

*adjectives commonly used with *me resulta* (positive): **agradable** (*pleasant*), **atractiv@** (*attractive/appealing*), **cómod@** (*comfortable/convenient*), **entrañable** (*pleasant*), **fascinante** (*fascinating*), **gracios@** (*funny*), **seductor/a** (*seductive*); (negative): **aburrid@** (*boring*), **deprimente** (*depressing*), **desagradable** (*unpleasant*), **incómod@** (*uncomfortable/awkward*), **monóton@** (*monotonous/boring*), **ofensiv@** (*offensive*), **pesad@** (*boring*), **violent@** (*awkward/embarrassing*)

Slang Flash

As in English, slang is very common in Spanish when it comes to giving your opinion. But be careful: there's slang and there's slang. The slang terms below are divided into three categories: 1) ☺, colloquial terms used and/or accepted by everybody, 2) 😎, "soft" slang used a lot by younger people and accepted by everyone, and 3) 😈, potentially offensive "hard" slang, which should be limited to use among *amigos*.

☺	😎	😈	
genial	**guai** [SP]	**cojonudo** [SP]	
fenomenal	**bestial**	**de puta madre** [SP]	great/
divin@ [LA]	**alucinante**	**la hostia** [SP]	cool/
chévere [LA]	**brutal** [SP]	**la leche** [SP]	fantastic
bárbar@ [LA]	**lo máximo** [LA]		
pésim@ [LA]	**un bodrio**	**una mierda**	terrible/
un horror	**un asco**	**una puta mierda**	lousy
una castaña [SP]	**un rollo** [SP]	**un coñazo** [SP]	boring/ a pain

Common Lead-ins

En mi opinión,...	In my opinion, . . .
Para mí,...☺	If you ask me, . . .
es un actor estupendo	he's a great actor
es la mejor escritora hoy en día	she's the best writer living today
A mi forma de ver,...	The way I see it, . . .
Tal como lo veo,...	The way I see it, . . .
Según lo veo,...	The way I see it, . . .
Yo diría que...	I'd say . . .
no es probable	it's unlikely
no merece la pena	it's not worth it

Agreeing

Estoy de acuerdo (contigo).	I agree (with you).
Estoy contigo.☺	I'll go along with you on that./I'm with you.
Sí, es verdad.	Yes, it's true.
Sí, es cierto.	Yes, it's true.
Tienes (toda la) razón.	You're (totally) right.
Algo de razón tienes.	You're half right.
No cabe la menor duda.	There's no doubt about that.
Has dado en el clavo.	You've hit the nail on the head.

Short Phrases and Exclamations

¡Claro!	Yeah!/Of course!
Desde luego.	Of course./Absolutely./No doubt about it.
Efectivamente.	Exactly.
Justo.☺	Exactly./You said it.
¡Ni que lo digas!☺	That's for sure!
Por supuesto.	Of course.
¡Sí, señor!☺/¡Sí, señora!☺	You got it!/I'll second that!
¡Sin duda!	Without a doubt.
¡Ya lo creo!☻ [SP]	Yeah!/Absolutely!
Ya te digo.☻ [SP]	You can say that again.

Disagreeing
Direct

No estoy de acuerdo (contigo).	I don't agree (with you).
No opino lo mismo.	I don't feel the same way.
No lo veo así.	I don't see it that way.
Lo veo de otra forma.	I see it another way.
Me parece que no es así.	I don't think that's the way it is.
Estás (muy) equivocad@.	You're (really) wrong.
Te equivocas.	You're mistaken.
No tienes razón.	You're wrong.

The Parrot Method

ERES UN POCO REPETITIVO...   ¿ REPETITIVO ?

This method of disagreeing with someone is even more common in Spanish than in English. That is, you repeat what the other person has just said (often only the last word) with an intonation that's somewhere between a question and an exclamation. The parrot method has several advantages. Much like a raised eyebrow, it's not openly confrontational. Plus its knee-jerk brevity keeps things light and lively.

A: **Pepa es una persona**
  muy puntual.
B: **¿Puntual?**

Pepa's a very punctual
  person.
Punctual?

A: **Madrid es una ciudad**
  muy barata.
B: **¿Barata?**

Madrid's a very inexpensive
  city.
Inexpensive?

Tactful/Indirect

No creo.   I don't think so.
¿Tu crees?   Do you think so?
¿Estás segur@?   Are you sure?
No sé yo...☺   I don't know . . . /I'm not so
                                        sure . . .
No sé si estoy de acuerdo.   I don't know if I agree.
No estoy tan segur@.   I'm not so sure.
No estoy tan convencid@.   I'm not so convinced.
No lo tengo tan claro.   I'm not so certain.

Idiom Flash • ¡Qué va! ☺ [SP]

This expression is used a lot in Spain to disagree with or contradict what someone has just said. Apart from being short and spunky, it trips off the tongue very well.

A: **Madrid es más bonita que Barcelona.**	Madrid is more beautiful than Barcelona.
B: **¡Qué va!**	No way!
A: **¿Tu hermana no es pintora?**	Isn't your sister a painter?
B: **¡Qué va! Es fotógrafa.**	No way! She's a photographer.

Short Phrases and Exclamations

Todo lo contrario.	It's just the opposite./It's just the other way round.
¡En absoluto!	Absolutely not!
¡Para nada!☻	Not at all!
¡Qué va!☺ [SP]	No way!/Yeah, right!
¡Qué dices!☻ [SP]	What are you saying?/Are you nuts?
¡Estás loc@!☻ [SP]	You're crazy!

Impressions and Hunches

Me parece que...	It seems to me that . . . /It looks like . . .
Me temo que...	I'm afraid that . . .
Sospecho que...	I suspect that . . .
va a ganar las elecciones	he/she is going to win the election
ya no me quiere	he/she doesn't love me any more

Tengo la sensación de que...	I've got a feeling that . . .
Me da la sensación de que...	I've got a feeling that . . .
Me da que...☺	I've got a feeling that . . .
no te gusta el arte abstracto	you don't like abstract art
va a llover mañana	it's going to rain tomorrow
No me sorprendería que...	I wouldn't be surprised if . . .
No me extrañaría que...	I wouldn't be surprised if . . .
ganara un Oscar	he/she/it won an Oscar
estuviera mintiendo	he/she was lying

Changing Your Mind

Lo retiro.	I take that back.
Rectifico.	Let me correct that.
Me he equivocado.	I made a mistake./I'm mistaken.
He cambiado de idea.	I've changed my mind.
He cambiado de opinión.	I've changed my mind/opinion.
Te doy la razón.	You're right./You win.
Me has hecho cambiar de idea.	You've made me change my mind.
Me has hecho verlo de otra forma.	You've made me see the light.

On the Spot

A *You're talking to a friend. Fill in the blanks in your conversation.*

Amiga   ¿Qué (1) _____ de Madrid?

Tú   Me (2) _____ una ciudad maravillosa.

Amiga   A mí también.

Tú   Pero está muy cara ahora.

Amiga   ¡Ni que lo (3) _____! El coste de la vida ha subido mucho.

Tú   Y Barcelona, ¿la conoces?

Amiga   Sí. Para (4) _____, es más bonita que Madrid.

Tú   No cabe la menor (5) _____.

Amiga   Pero, bueno, Madrid tiene otra cosa.

Tú   (6) _____ de acuerdo. Tiene un encanto especial...

B *You and a friend are browsing in a bookstore. Fill in the blanks in your conversation.*

Amigo   ¿Conoces a este autor?

Tú   Sí, he leído algo de él.

Amigo   ¿Te (1) _____?

Tú   No mucho. Me (2) _____ un poco pesado.

Amigo   ¿(3) _____? ¡(4) _____ va! Es muy gracioso.

Tú   ¿Tú (5) _____?

Amigo   Sí. Mira, lee este libro. Ya verás cómo te ríes.

Tú   Vale. A ver si me hace cambiar de (6) _____.

9

Giving Descriptions

Mark and Pepa chat in a café.

Mark	¿Cómo describirías a Lola?
Pepa	¿Cómo la describiría?
Mark	Sí. ¿Cómo es?
Pepa	¡Pero si ya la conoces!
Mark	Ya, pero quiero tu opinión.
Pepa	A ver... Pues es inteligente, graciosa, sensible...
Mark	¿Sensible? Eso me sorprende. Parece muy poco práctica.
Pepa	Hombre, de práctica no tiene nada. Pero eso no tiene nada que ver.
Mark	¿Cómo?
Pepa	Que Lola es muy delicada. Le afectan mucho las cosas.
Mark	¡Ah! Ya veo lo que dices.
Pepa	Por eso está la pobre como una cabra.
Mark	¿Eh?
Pepa	¡Que es una broma! Es una bellísima persona.
Mark	Sí que lo es. Y encima es guapísima...
Pepa	Bueno, más que guapa, yo diría que es atractiva.
Mark	Tienes razón.
Pepa	Y además es alta y tiene buen tipo...
Mark	Es verdad, es muy alta. ¿Cuánto mide?
Pepa	No sé, un metro setenta y algo.
Mark	Eso en pies, ¿cuánto es?
Pepa	¿En pies? Ni idea. Oye, estás loquito por Lola, ¿no?
Mark	¿Por qué? ¿Se me nota?

ES UNA BELLÍSIMA PERSONA...

Mark	How would you describe Lola?
Pepa	**How would I describe her?**
Mark	Yeah. **What's she like?**
Pepa	But you know her!
Mark	**I know**, but I want your opinion.
Pepa	**Let's see** . . . Well, she's **intelligent, funny, sensitive** . . . [NOT *sensible*]
Mark	*Sensitive?* (which he thinks means *sensible*) That surprises me. She seems **a little impractical** to me.
Pepa	You're right, **she's about as impractical as you can get**. But **that's got nothing to do with it**.
Mark	What?
Pepa	I just mean that Lola's very delicate. Things really affect her.
Mark	Oh! **I get it now.**
Pepa	That's why **the poor thing's nutty as a fruitcake**.
Mark	Huh?
Pepa	It's a joke! **She's a really beautiful person.**
Mark	**She certainly is.** And what's more **she's really pretty**.
Pepa	Well, **rather than pretty, I'd say she's attractive**.
Mark	You're right.
Pepa	And what's more, **she's tall and has a good body**.
Mark	It's true, **she's very tall. How tall is she?**
Pepa	I don't know, one meter seventy-something.
Mark	What's that in feet?
Pepa	In feet? **No idea**. Hey, you're crazy about Lola, right?
Mark	Why? **Does it show?**

Asking for a Description

¿Cómo es...?	What's . . . like?
Dime cómo es...	Tell me what . . . is like.
Cuéntame cómo es...	Tell me what . . . is like.
tu amig@	your friend
tu herman@	your brother/sister
¿Cómo describirías a...?	How would you describe . . . ?
¿Qué aspecto tiene...?	What does . . . look like?
¿Cómo es (físicamente)...?	What does . . . look like?
tu prim@	your cousin
tu vecin@	your neighbor

Describing Someone Physically

Es...	He's/She's . . .
alt@	tall
baj@ or bajit@	short
de estatura media	medium-height
joven	young
mayor	old
de aspecto juvenil	youthful
atractiv@	attractive
fe@ or [SP] feúch@	ugly
guap@	handsome/beautiful
delgad@	thin
flac@	skinny
fuerte	well-built
gord@ or gordit@	fat
grandote/a	big
calv@	bald
moren@	dark
pelirroj@	a redhead
rubi@	blond

Eyes

Tiene (los) ojos...	He's/She's got . . . eyes.
azules	blue
marrones	brown
negros	black
verdes	green
verdosos	hazel

~~~~~~

Suffix Flash • -it@

Yes, the diminutive suffix **-it@** indicates smallness (**una casita** = *a little house*), but it can also convey fondness or affection. And, if you're describing how someone is physically, it takes the edge off "negative" adjectives like **bajo** or **gordo**.

Es bajo.	He's short.	**Es bajito.**	He's a little guy.
Es gorda.	She's fat.	**Es gordita.**	She's on the plump side.

~~~~~~

Hair

Tiene el pelo...	He's/She's got . . . hair.
corto	short
largo	long
rapado	very short (*crew cut*)
liso	straight
ondulado	wavy
rizado	curly
canoso	gray
castaño	chestnut
moreno	brown
negro	black
rubio	blond
teñido (de malva)	dyed (mauve)

Other Defining Features

Tiene...	He's/She's got . . .
barba	a beard
bigote	a moustache
canas	gray hair
entradas	a receding hairline
melena	a mane (*long, thick hair*)
patillas	sideburns
una buena nariz	a "good" (*big*) nose
facciones fuertes	strong features
la nariz chata	a snub nose
los ojos saltones	bug eyes

una cicatriz	a scar
un lunar	a mole
pecas	freckles
barriga	a big belly
buen tipo	a good figure/body
los hombros anchos	broad shoulders
las piernas largas	long legs
un tatuaje	a tattoo
un piercing en el ombligo	a pierced navel
Lleva...	He/She wears/has . . .
coleta	a pony-tail
gafas [SP]/lentes [LA]	glasses
peluca	a wig
trenzas	braids

For physical descriptions of places and things, see pages 170–171 in the Word Bank.

Cranking It Up • -ísim@

This golden suffix cranks adjectives up to a higher pitch, and is more emphatic than its alternative—that is, using **muy** with the adjective. Best of all, **-ísim@** slides off the tongue with great ease and flair. Try it. With a little practice, you'll find it's *facilísimo*.

Es (muy) guapa.	She's (really) pretty.
Es guapísima.	She's gorgeous.
Es (muy) divertido.	He's (a lot of) fun.
Es divertidísimo.	He's a riot.
Es (muy) fácil.	It's (really) easy.
Es facilísimo.	It's a cinch.

Describing Personality

Es (muy)...	He's/She's (very) . . .
abiert@	open, communicative
alegre	cheerful, upbeat
amable	kind
ambicios@	ambitious
ansios@	anxious, nervous
aventurer@	adventurous
borde☺ [SP]	rude, stroppy
buena gente☺	a good person
cabezota☺ [SP]	stubborn
cálid@	warm
callad@	quiet
cariños@	warm, affectionate
cerrad@	reserved, uncommunicative
coquet@	vain, flirtatious
crític@	critical
de fiar	trustworthy, reliable
despistad@	scatterbrained, forgetful
discret@	discreet
divertid@	fun
dulce	kind, sweet
egoísta	selfish, self-centered
envidios@	envious
exigente	demanding
frí@	cold
generos@	generous
histéric@	hysterical
indecis@	indecisive
independiente	independent
ingenu@	naïve
inquiet@	restless
insegur@	insecure
inteligente	intelligent
interesante	interesting
legal☺ [SP]	trustworthy, honest
list@	clever

marchos@ [SP]	lively/a party animal
mentiros@	a liar
neurótic@	neurotic
ocios@ [LA]	lazy
orgullos@	proud
prepotente	arrogant
sensat@	sensible
sincer@	honest
soberbi@	proud, haughty
sociable	sociable
sos@	dull
tacañ@	stingy, miserly
terc@ [LA]	stubborn
tiern@	tender, loving
tímid@	shy
tont@	stupid, silly
trabajador/a	hard-working
tranquil@	calm, laid back
vital	lively, dynamic

False Friend Alert!

Watch out for adjectives related to personality. If you're not careful, you can get thrown off by some major false friends here. Here are a few common ones:

espléndid@	generous (with money)
extravagante	flamboyant
formal [SP]	reliable, decent
gracios@	funny
informal [SP]	unreliable, easy come easy go
inocente	naïve
interesad@	out for himself/herself
maniátic@	fussy, finicky, fanatical
nervios@	hyper, high-strung
presumid@	vain
rar@	strange, weird
sensible	sensitive
simpátic@	friendly, nice
vag@	lazy

Common Expressions

No es muy (listo).	He's not very (clever).
Es muy poco (práctica).	She's not very (practical).
No es nada (tímida).	She's not at all (shy).
De (simpático) no tiene nada.	He's not (nice) at all.
De tonto no tiene ni un pelo.☺	There isn't a stupid hair on his head.
Más que (inteligente), yo diría que es (listo).	Rather than (intelligent), I'd say he's (clever).

Es...

He's/She's . . .

una bellísima persona	a wonderful person
un/a buenaz@ [SP]	a really good person
un caradura☺	cheeky, got a lot of nerve
un cerebro [SP]	brilliant, extremely intelligent
un/a cotilla☺ [SP]	a gossip
un/a chismos@ [LA]	a gossip
un/a juerguista	a party animal
un/a listill@☺ [SP]	a wise guy
un/a payas@	a clown
una persona normal	normal (*that is, not strange*)
un personaje	a real character
un/a sinvergüenza	shameless

Tiene...

He's/She's (got) . . .

buen carácter	good-natured, easy-going
mal carácter	difficult, moody
mucho carácter	a strong character
(mucho *or* mal) genio	a (bad) temper
(mucha) gracia	(very) funny
mucha labia	the gift of gab
(muy) mala leche☻ [SP]	a (really) mean streak
(mucha) picardía	crafty, cunning (*usually positive*)

Es una persona llamativa.	He's/She's someone you notice.
Llama la atención.	He/She stands out./You notice him/her.
Le gusta llamar la atención.	He/She likes to be noticed.

Idiom Flash • estar como una cabra ☺ [SP]

ESTÁS COMO UNA CABRA

This expression, which is used a lot in Spain, literally means *to be like a she-goat*. Another variation is *estar como una regadera*—literally, *to be like a watering can*. Meanwhile, in Latin America, go with *estar chiflad@* if you want to say someone is a little loony, nuts, or not all there.

Note that these expressions are used with *estar* (and not *ser*), and so refer to passing or circumstantial madness rather than a permanent state of insanity. Also, like *estar loc@*, they're often used lightly or teasingly among *amigos*.

Useful Phrases

A ver...	Let's see./Let me think.
Eso no tiene nada que ver.	That's got nothing to do with it.
Ni idea.	I've got no idea.
¿Se me nota?	Does it show?/Is it really obvious?
Sí que lo es.	He/She/It certainly is.
Ya. ☺ [SP]	I know.
Ya (lo) sé.	I know (it).
Ya veo lo que dices.	I get it now./I see what you mean.

On the Spot

A *You ask Pepa to describe Pili. Fill in the blanks in your conversation. (Except for number 5, take your cue from the words in parentheses.)*

Tú	¿Cómo es Pili?
Pepa	¿No la conoces? Pues es un (1) _____ *(real character)*.
Tú	¿Ah, sí? Cuéntame cómo es...
Pepa	A ver... ¿Cómo la describiría? Es (2) _____ *(friendly)*, (3) _____ *(fun)*, un poco (4) _____ *(flamboyant)*.
Tú	¿Ah, sí? ¿Le gusta llamar la (5) _____?
Pepa	Mucho. Y luego te ríes mucho con ella. Es muy (6) _____ *(funny)*.

B *Pili asks Lola to describe her cousin, Paco. Fill in the blanks in your conversation. (Take your cue from the words in parentheses.)*

Pili	¿Cómo es tu primo?
Lola	¿Paco? Pues es muy inteligente, (1) _____ *(warm)*, sociable... Y luego es una persona muy (2) _____ *(independent)* e (3) _____ *(restless)*.
Pili	Ajá. Y físicamente, ¿cómo es?
Lola	Pues es (4) _____ *(short)*, un poco (5) _____ *(fat)*, con los ojos saltones.
Pili	Así que no es ningún Adonis...
Lola	En absoluto. Pero mira, curiosamente es un tío muy (6) _____ *(attractive)*.

10

Relaying News and Gossip

Pepa and Pili meet up the next day.

Pili   **¿Sabes lo de** Lola?

Pepa   **¿Lo de** Lola?

Pili   **¿No te has enterado?**

Pepa   No, **no sé nada**. ¿Qué ha pasado?

Pili   Anoche tuvo un accidente.

Pepa   **¿De verdad?** ¿Pero está bien?

Pili   Sí, **acabo de hablar con ella**. **Por lo visto** no fue grave.

Pepa   **Menos mal.**

Pili   Pero tiene que quedarse en el hospital un par de días.

Pepa   **Vaya...** Y el accidente, **¿cómo fue?**

Pili   Un coche le dio por detrás. **Parece ser que** el conductor estaba borracho perdido.

Pepa   **¡Qué horror!**

Pili   Bueno, **y no te lo pierdas**, **corre la voz de que** era el hermano del ex-novio de la cuñada del príncipe.

Pepa   ¿Eh?

Pili   **Que sí**, el ex-novio de la cuñada del príncipe tiene dos hermanos. Éste es el mayor. **Dicen que** no está bien de la cabeza...Y, **según las malas lenguas**, está metido en el contrabando de armas.

Pepa   **¿Qué dices?**

Pili   **Lo que oyes**. En fin, **creo que** tiene una pequeña fortuna. Aparte de un chalé en la sierra, otro en la costa, un par de barcos de vela y un avión privado.

Pepa   **¡Qué barbaridad!**

Pili   **Eso digo yo**. En fin, ¿tú cómo andas? **Cuéntame...**

Pili	**Do you know about** Lola?
Pepa	**About** Lola?
Pili	**Haven't you heard?**
Pepa	**No, I don't know anything.** What happened?
Pili	She had a car accident last night.
Pepa	**Really?** And is she OK?
Pili	Yeah, **I just spoke with her. Apparently** it wasn't serious.
Pepa	**Thank God for that.**
Pili	But she has to stay in the hospital for a couple of days.
Pepa	**Oh dear...** And **how did** the accident **happen?**
Pili	A car hit her from behind. **It seems** the driver was totally drunk.
Pepa	**That's awful!**
Pili	Well, **and get this, word has it** he's the brother of the prince's sister-in-law's ex-boyfriend.
Pepa	Huh?
Pili	**I swear it's true.** The prince's sister-in-law's ex-boyfriend has two brothers. This one's the older one. **From what I hear**, he's not all there. **And rumor has it** he's involved in arms smuggling.
Pepa	**Are you serious?**
Pili	**I'm not kidding.** Anyway, **I believe** he has a small fortune. Apart from a house in the mountains, another on the coast, a couple of sailboats, and a private plane.
Pepa	**Good God!**
Pili	**That's what I say.** Anyway, what's up with you? **Fill me in.**

News/Gossip Preludes

¿Has oído la noticia?	Have you heard the news?
¿Te has enterado? [SP]	Have you heard?/Do you know?
¿Estás al tanto?	Have you heard the latest?
¿Estás al corriente?	Have you heard the latest?
¿Has oído...?	Have you heard . . . ?
¿Sabes...?	Do you know . . . ?
¿Te has enterado de...? [SP]	Have you heard . . . ?
lo de (Lola)	about (Lola)
lo del terremoto	about the earthquake
¿A que no sabes...?	I bet you don't know . . .
¿A que no te has enterado de...? [SP]	I bet you haven't heard . . .
lo de (Lola)	about (Lola)
los resultados	the results

Key Lead-in • Lo de...

This is a great little crutch when you want to refer to something quickly, and is indispensable for relaying news or gossip. **Lo de...** literally means *the thing of . . .*, but, depending on the context, it could be translated as *the latest about . . .* or *the scoop on . . .*

¿Sabes lo de Lola?	Do you know about Lola?
¿Estás al tanto de lo del terremoto?	Are you up on the whole earthquake thing?

Responding

Affirmative

Sí...	Yes . . .
acabo de oír la noticia	I've just heard the news
me acabo de enterar [SP]	I've just found out
me lo acaban de contar	I've just been told
me lo ha dicho (Pili)	(Pili) told me
no es ningún secreto	it's no secret
lo he oído en la radio	I heard it on the radio
lo he visto en el telediario	I saw it on the news
ya me lo han dicho	I've already been told

Negative

¿Cómo?	What?
¿De qué hablas?	What are you talking about?
¿Qué noticia?	What news?
¿Qué ha pasado?	What happened?
No...	No . . .
ni idea☺	I'm clueless
no sé nada	I don't know anything
nadie me ha dicho nada	nobody's told me anything
no he visto el telediario hoy	I haven't watched the news today
no he leído la prensa hoy	I haven't read the paper today

Grammar Flash • *acabar de* + infinitive

Since *acabar de* + the infinitive is used to refer to something that's *just* happened or *just* been done, it's a common way of prefacing and relaying news.

Acabo de oírlo en la radio.	I've just heard it on the radio.
El presidente acaba de dimitir.	The president's just resigned.
Un avión acaba de estrellarse.	There's just been a plane crash.

Relaying News Headlines

El Papa ha tenido un infarto.	The Pope's had a heart attack.
Han asesinado al líder de la oposición.	The leader of the opposition's been assassinated.
Han secuestrado a la hija del rey.	They've kidnapped the king's daughter.
Han subido los tipos de interés.	They've raised interest rates.
La bolsa ha caído en picado.	The stock market's crashed.
Ha habido...	There's been . . .
un accidente	an accident
un apagón	a blackout
un atentado	a terrorist attack
un huracán	a hurricane
un incendio	a fire
una insurrección	an uprising
una inundación	a flood
una matanza	a massacre
un terremoto	an earthquake

Relaying Gossip and Secondhand Information

Creo que...	I believe (that) . . .
Dicen que...	They say (that) . . .
He oído que...	I've heard (that) . . .
Me han dicho que...	I've been told (that) . . .
Resulta que...	It turns out (that) . . . /It just so happens (that) . . .
Según dicen/cuentan...	According to what they say . . .
está forrado☺ [SP]	he's loaded
es transexual	she's a transsexual
pega a su mujer	he's a wife beater
se dedica al contrabando	he's into smuggling
Corre la voz de que...	Word has it (that) . . .
Parece ser que...	It seems (that) . . .
Por lo visto...	Apparently . . .
Se rumorea que...	It's rumored (that) . . .

Según las malas lenguas...	Rumor has it (that) . . .
lo van a dejar☺ [SP]	they're going to split up
Olga está embarazada	Olga's pregnant
Juan se ha fugado con otra	Juan's gone off with another woman
María se ha hecho mormona	Maria's become a Mormon

~~~~~~~~

Culture Flash • The Spanish Grapevine

Time to go to the market to get some fruit and vegetables. Today you're in luck. There's only one lady ahead of you, and she's just finishing up. As he weighs her order of tomatoes, the fruit stand vendor asks about the woman's nephew, who just got out of the hospital. Twenty minutes later, you're still waiting. Now they're dishing the dirt on a local celebrity ("Oh, and I forgot! Give me a couple of lemons too"), whose main claim to fame is a brief affair with a playboy distantly related to the Spanish royal family.

Yes, gossip is a major pastime in the Spanish-speaking world. Every hairdresser's and doctor's office in Spain has a copy of *Hola* magazine (the best-selling gossip rag) lying around. And then there's garden-variety gossip, which half the time isn't even called gossip. It's just shooting the breeze, and taking a healthy interest in the lives of all those people you know. And why not? After all, a little juicy scoop is always entertaining.

~~~~~~~~

Responding

¿De verdad?	Really?
¡No me lo creo!	I don't believe it!
¡Qué fuerte!☻	That's incredible!/That's too much!
Vaya...	Well, well./Get a load of that./Oh, my!
¡Qué barbaridad!☺	Good God!
¡Qué horror!	That's awful!
¡Qué le vamos a hacer!☺	Oh well, what can you do?/That's too bad!
¿Cómo fue?	How did it happen?
Cuéntame.	Tell me./Fill me in.
No creo que sea verdad.	I don't think that's true.
Se lo habrán inventado.	I don't believe that./They must have made that up.
Será un rumor.	It must be a rumor.

For more expressions, see "Showing Surprise or Disbelief" on page 28 in Unit 3, "Breaking the Ice."

Common Phrases

En serio.	Seriously.
Eso digo yo.	That's what I say.
Lo que oyes.☺	You better believe it./I'm not joking.
Menos mal.	Just as well./Thank God for that.
No es ninguna broma.	It's no joke.
¡No te lo pierdas!☺	Get this!/Get a load of this!
Sin bromear.	I'm not kidding.
Te lo juro.	I swear to God.
Que sí.☻ [SP]	I swear it's true. (*used for emphasis or else to contradict sb*)

Relaying Personal News
Good News

He aprobado el examen.	I passed the exam.
He encontrado un trabajo.	I've found a job.
Me han ascendido.	I've been given a promotion.
Soy tí@.	I've just become an uncle/aunt.

Bad News

Ha fallecido mi abuela.	My grandma's passed away.
Me han suspendido.	I failed (the exam).
Me han robado el monedero.	My wallet's been stolen.
No me han renovado el contrato.	They didn't renew my contract.

~~~~~~~~

Slang Flash • ¡Qué putada! ⊚ [SP]

This is the Spanish equivalent of *What a bummer!* or *That sucks!* Since it's very informal, reserve *¡qué putada!* for use among *amigos,* and just to respond to minor calamities. It's definitely *not* appropriate as a response to news of a serious illness or death, or anything amounting to a real tragedy.

A: Le han echado a Juan del trabajo.	Juan's been fired.
B: ¡Qué putada!	What a bummer!
A: Se me ha averiado el coche.	My car's broken down.
B: ¡Qué putada!	What a bummer!
But...	
A: Ha fallecido mi madre.	My mother's passed away.
B: ~~¡Qué putada!~~ Lo siento muchísimo.	I'm so sorry.
A: Se ha estrellado un avión.	There's been a plane crash.
B: ~~¡Qué putada!~~ ¡Qué horror!	That's awful!

Responding
Good News

¡Cuánto me alegro!	Good for you!/I'm so glad to hear that!
¡Enhorabuena!	Congratulations!
Me alegro (mucho).	I'm (really) glad to hear that.
¡Qué bien!	That's great!
¡Qué buena noticia!	That's great news!
Te lo mereces.	You deserve it.

Bad News

¡Ánimo!	Keep your chin up!/Don't let it get you down!
¡Cuánto lo siento!	I'm so sorry!
Lo siento mucho.	I'm really sorry (to hear that).
¡Qué putada!☺ [SP]	That sucks!/What a bummer!
Vaya.	That's too bad./Oh, dear.

On the Spot

A *You and Pepa are chatting. Fill in the blanks in your conversation.*

Pepa   ¿Has (1) _____ lo del incendio?

Tú   ¿Qué incendio?

Pepa   ¿No te has (2) _____?

Tú   No, ni (3) _____.

Pepa   Pues ha habido un incendio enorme en la sierra.

Tú   ¿Ah, sí? ¡Qué (4) _____! ¿Y cómo pasó?

Pepa   Pues por lo (5) _____ fue el acto de un pirómano.

Tú   Ajá. ¿Pero no se ha muerto nadie?

Pepa   No, no ha llegado a ninguna casa.

Tú   Menos (6) _____.

Pepa   Sí, pero se ha quedado todo el monte negro.

Tú   (7) _____.

B *Pepa and Pili continue chatting. Fill in the blanks in their conversation.*

Pili   Por cierto, ¿sabes (1)_____ de Paco?

Pepa   ¿Qué Paco?

Pili   Paco, el primo de Lola.

Pepa   ¡Ah! No, no sé (2)_____. Cuéntame.

Pili   Se ha hecho mormón.

Pepa   ¡No me lo (3)_____!

Pili   Te lo juro, me lo (4)_____ de contar.

Pepa   ¡(5)_____ fuerte!

Pili   Y ahora (6)_____ ser que se va a casar con otra.

Pepa   ¿Cómo?

Pili   No es ninguna broma. Ya sabes que los mormones pueden tener varias mujeres.

Pepa   Es verdad. ¿Y quién es la otra mujer?

Pili   Pues, no te lo (7)_____, la ex-novia de su cuñado.

Pepa   ¿La rubita esa que trabaja en la clínica veterinaria?

Pili   Sí, esa misma...

11

Saying How You Feel

Mark and Pepa visit Lola at the hospital.

Pepa	Hola, Lola.
Lola	¡Pepa! ¡Qué sorpresa!
Pepa	¿Cómo te encuentras?
Lola	**Mucho mejor.** Creo que el lunes **me dan el alta.**
Pepa	¿Tan rápido?
Lola	Sí, **la lesión no era nada grave.** Ya está casi curada.
Pepa	Estupendo. Y de ánimo, ¿cómo andas? ¿Se te ha pasado el susto?
Lola	Más o menos. Vaya loco...

(Entra Mark.)

Mark	Hola. Bueno, ¿y de qué loco estabais hablando? Espero que no de mí...
Lola	Que no, tonto. Del conductor del otro coche.
Mark	¡Ah, ese cerdo! Si le veo, le digo un par de cosas.
Lola	Y yo. Gracias a él, ahora sólo la idea de subir a un coche **me da pánico.**
Mark	No lo pienses de momento. En fin, ¿cómo estás?
Lola	**Un poco depre. Estoy hasta el moño** de estar aquí.
Mark	Normal. ¿Y por lo demás?
Lola	**Bien. Me duele un poco el cuello,** pero **estoy casi recuperada.**
Mark	Me alegro mucho. Y tú, Pepa, ¿qué tal?
Pepa	**Un poco pachucha.** Llevo días **constipada.**
Mark	¡Qué asco! No seas tan indiscreta.
Pepa	¿Qué pasa? ¿Nunca has tenido **un resfriado?**
Mark	¿Eh?
Pepa	Anda, pásame ese kleenex, que **me tengo que sonar.**

ME DA PÁNICO...

Pepa	Hi, Lola.
Lola	Pepa! **What a surprise!**
Pepa	**How are you feeling?**
Lola	**Much better.** I think **they'll be letting me out** on Monday.
Pepa	So fast?
Lola	Yeah, **it wasn't a serious injury. It's almost healed now.**
Pepa	Great. **And emotionally, how do you feel? Have you gotten over the shock?**
Lola	More or less. What a madman . . .

(Mark comes in.)

Mark	Hello. So, what madman were you talking about? Not me, I hope . . .
Lola	No, silly. The driver of the other car.
Mark	Oh, that jerk! If I see him, I'll give him a piece of my mind.
Lola	Me too. Thanks to him, just the idea of getting into a car now **freaks me out.**
Mark	Don't think about it right now. Anyway, **how are you?**
Lola	**A little down. I'm fed up with** being here.
Mark	That's normal. And apart from that?
Lola	**Good. My neck hurts a little**, but **I'm almost back to normal.**
Mark	I'm glad to hear that. And, Pepa, **how are you?**
Pepa	**A little under the weather. I've had a cold** [NOT *I've been constipated*] for days.
Mark	**That's disgusting!** Don't be so indiscreet.
Pepa	What's the matter? Haven't you ever had **a cold?**
Mark	Huh?
Pepa	Come on, pass me that Kleenex, **I have to blow my nose.**

103

Asking How Someone Feels

¿Cómo estás?	
¿Qué tal (estás)?	} How are you?
¿Cómo andas? ☺ [SP]	

¿Cómo te encuentras?	How are you feeling? (*physical state*)
¿Cómo te sientes?	How are you feeling? (*emotional state*)
¿Estás mejor?	Are you better?
¿Te encuentras mejor?	Are you feeling better?
¿Te sientes mejor?	Are you feeling better?

Saying How You Feel Physically

Estoy...	I'm . . . /I feel . . .
Me encuentro...	I feel . . .

Positive		**Negative**	
bien	well	baj@ de energía	low-energy, weak
con más energía	more energetic	débil *or* floj@ ☺ [SP]	weak
en plena forma	in top form	fastidiad@ ☺ [SP]	not in great shape
(mucho) mejor	(much) better		
(casi) recuperad@	(almost) recovered, back to normal	mal	bad
		mal@ *or* malit@	sick
		regular	not great

Common Expressions

Estoy...	I'm . . . /I feel . . .
hech@ una pena ☺ [SP]	like a wreck, terrible
(un poco) pachuch@ ☺ [SP]	(a little) under the weather
No estoy.../No me encuentro...	I'm not feeling . . .
muy allá ☺	great
muy católic@ ☺ [SP]	very good

For general responses about how you are, see page 5 in Unit 1.

False Friend Alert!

It's winter, and all your *amigos* are suddenly complaining about being *constipados*. Don't be alarmed: it's not what it sounds like. **Estoy constipad@** is just another way to say you have a cold, along with **tengo un resfriado** or **tengo un catarro**. FYI: *I'm constipated* is **estoy estreñid@**.

Checking in on an Ailing Pal

¿Cómo estás (del estómago)?	How's (your stomach)?
¿Qué tal (la alergia)?	How's (your allergy)?
¿Cómo va (esa pierna)?	How's (that leg) doing?
¿Sigues...?	Do you still have . . . ?
con alergia	your allergy
con dolor	pain
con gripe	the flu
constipad@	a cold
¿Se te ha pasado...?	Has . . . gone/eased up?
¿Se te ha quitado...?	Has . . . gone away?
el dolor de cabeza	your headache
el dolor de espalda	your back pain
la fiebre	your fever/temperature
el mareo	the dizziness
¿Estás tomando algo?	Are you taking anything? (*i.e., medicine*)
¿Has ido al médico?	Have you gone to the doctor?
¿Qué te ha dicho el médico?	What did the doctor say?
¿Te han recetado algo?	Did they give you a prescription?

Talking About Pain and Discomfort

Me duele...	. . . hurts
el cuello	My neck
la garganta	My throat
la tripa☺ [SP]	My tummy
Me molesta...	. . . is bothering me
el brazo	My arm
la espalda	My back
la pierna	My leg
Tengo dolor de...	I have a . . . ache
cabeza	head
estómago	stomach
muelas	tooth

For more parts of the body, see pages 166–167 in the Word Bank.

For more physical symptoms, see pages 165–166 in the Word Bank.

Common Remarks

¡Au! *or* ¡Ay! *or* ¡Ay, ay, ay!	Ouch!
Me duele (mucho/un poco).	It hurts (a lot/a little).
Me molesta (mucho/un poco).	It's bothering me (a lot/a little).
Es incómodo.	It's uncomfortable.
Espero que se me pase.	I hope it goes away.
No es grave.	It isn't serious.
No es nada./No ha sido nada.	It's nothing.
Es una chorrada.☻ [SP]	It's no big deal.
No tiene importancia.	It's nothing./It isn't serious.
Ya se me pasará.	It'll go away soon.
Ya no me duele.	It doesn't hurt anymore.
Ya se me va pasando.	It's going away.
Se está curando.	It's healing.
Está curad@.	It's healed.
Me van a dar el alta.	I'm going to be released (*from the hospital*).

~~~~~~

Culture Flash • Aches and Pains

Your friend's just told you she's *constipada*. You're a little grossed out, but then relax and realize she just has a common cold. After going into excruciating detail about sinus congestion and mucus buildup, she pauses and then proceeds to tell you about the malfunctioning of her digestive tract. Your initial alarm returns full force. Apart from that cold, she's also constipated and (gag!) talking about it freely.

No, your *amiga* is not a weirdo. She simply reflects a general national obsession (in Spain, that is—Latin Americans are a little more discreet on this front) with one's bodily functions. Damn right: up there with soccer, food, and the family, one's physical state is a major standby conversation topic in Spain, and no body part or symptom is off limits. What's more, if you go pale or pass out at any point, you'll be met with an indulgent smile and a quip about the puritanical American character.

Your *amiga*'s finally finished up with her account. It's your call now, and you're suddenly aware you have a splitting headache, and you're backside's a bit numb from sitting on that wooden chair. You may as well tell her all about it. If you can't beat 'em, join 'em!

~~~~~~

Saying How You Feel Emotionally

Estoy (muy)...		I'm (really) . . . /I feel (really) . . .
Me siento...		I'm feeling . . .

Positive		**Negative**	
a gusto	happy, comfortable	agobiad@ [SP]	overwhelmed, stressed out
bien	good	asustad@	shaken up, alarmed
centrad@	centered		
content@	happy	baj@ de ánimo	down

divinamente☺	great	**cabread@**☻ [SP]	pissed off
emocionad@	excited, really happy	**de mal humor**	in a bad mood
		decepcionad@	disappointed
en las nubes☺	on cloud nine	**deprimid@** or	down,
encantad@	delighted (with *sb/st*)	**depre**☻	depressed
		desanimad@	discouraged
estupendamente	great	**descentrad@**	uncentered, off-kilter
feliz	happy		
fenomenal☻ [SP]	great	**disgustad@**	upset
inspirad@	inspired	**enfadad@**	angry
motivad@	motivated	**enojad@** [LA]	annoyed
satisfech@	satisfied	**hart@**	fed up
tranquil@	calm	**preocupad@**	worried
		quemad@☻ [SP]	burned out
		triste	sad

Showing Concern

¿**Cómo andas de ánimo?**
¿**Cómo estás de ánimo?**
¿**Qué tal estás de ánimo?**
	How are your spirits?/
	  Emotionally, how do
	  you feel?

¿**Sigues...?**	Are you still . . . ?
cabread@☻ [SP]	pissed off
deprimid@	depressed/down
disgustad@	upset
¿**Se te ha pasado el cabreo?**☻ [SP]*	Have you cooled off?/Are you still angry?
¿**Se te ha pasado la depre?**☻ [SP]*	Are you feeling any better? (*that is, less depressed*)
¿**Se te ha pasado el disgusto?***	Are you feeling less upset?
¿**Se te ha pasado el susto?***	Are you still shaken up?/Have you gotten over the shock?

---

*¿*Se te ha pasado...?* basically means *Have you gotten over (your anger, depression,* and so on)? Here we've provided the most common English equivalents.

Idiom Flash • ¡Estoy hasta...!

ESTOY HASTA LAS NARICES

Fed up? You've got loads of options in Spanish for saying you've had it. Apart from **estoy hart@**, there's a whole slew of colorful phrases kicking off with **Estoy hasta...** (*I'm up to . . .*). We've listed them below with their literal translations, just for kicks.

¡Estoy hasta la coronilla!☺	I'm up to the crown of my head!
¡Estoy hasta el gorro!☺ [SP]	I'm up to my cap!
¡Estoy hasta los huevos!☻ [SP]	I'm up to my balls! (*vulgar; mostly used by men*)
¡Estoy hasta el moño!☺ [SP]	I'm up to my hair bun! (*mostly used by women*)
¡Estoy hasta las narices!☻ [SP]	I'm up to my noses! (*yes, this is plural . . .*)

Blowing It Off

Ya se me ha pasado.	I've gotten over it./It's blown over.
Fue una cosa momentánea.	It was just a passing thing.
Fue una tontería.	It was nothing.
No tiene importancia.	It was nothing.
Está olvidado.	I've forgotten about it.

Gut Reactions • *me da + a feeling*

This is a common way of saying that something makes you feel something—that is, it causes an emotional and/or physical reaction. **Me da miedo**, for example, literally means *It gives me fear,* that is, *It's scary.* Some other common combinations:

Me da alegría.	It makes me happy.
Me da asco.	It makes me feel sick./It's disgusting.
Me da envidia.	It makes me green with envy.
Me da hambre.	It makes me hungry.
Me da morbo. ☺ [SP]	It's a turn-on. (*sexually*)
Me da pánico.	It freaks me out.
Me da pena.	It makes me sad.
Me da rabia.	It annoys/infuriates me.
Me da repelús.	It gives me the heebie-jeebies/creeps.
Me da risa.	It cracks me up.
Me da sed.	It makes me thirsty.
Me da sueño.	It makes me sleepy/drowsy.

Finally, there's the informal **Me da algo**☺—literally, *it gives me "something."* This covers quite a lot of terrain: *I don't feel right about it* or *I don't feel comfortable with it* or *it makes me feel uneasy/upset/awkward.*

Common Exclamations

¡Qué alegría!	Wow!/Great!/Yay!
¡Qué alivio!	What a relief!
¡Qué asco!	That's disgusting!/Gross!/Yuck!
¡Qué envidia!	Lucky you! I'm green with envy!
¡Qué miedo!	That's really scary!
¡Qué morbo! ☺ [SP]	That's a real turn-on!

¡Qué pena!	What a pity!
¡Qué rabia!	How annoying!/What a bummer!/What a bitch!
¡Qué risa!	How funny!/What a riot!
¡Qué sorpresa!	What a surprise!

On the Spot

A   *Lola and Mark continue chatting in the hospital. Fill in the blanks in their conversation.*

Mark   ¿Así que te (1)＿＿＿＿＿＿＿＿ bien?

Lola   Sí, no ha sido (2)＿＿＿＿＿＿＿＿ la lesión.

Mark   Me alegro. Estaba preocupado.

Lola   Lo que (3)＿＿＿＿＿＿＿＿ molesta es no poder moverme.

Mark   Claro. Oye, ya que estamos solos, te quería preguntar algo.

Lola   Dime.

Mark   ¿Se te ha (4)＿＿＿＿＿＿＿＿ el cabreo conmigo?

Lola   ¡Ah, eso! Claro. No (5)＿＿＿＿＿＿＿＿ importancia.

Mark   ¿Seguro?

Lola   Sí, no te preocupes. (6)＿＿＿＿＿＿＿＿ olvidado.

B   *You phone a friend who's got the flu. Fill in the blanks in your conversation.*

Tú   ¿Qué tal (1)＿＿＿＿＿＿＿＿?

Amiga   Pues sigo un poco pachucha.

Tú   ¿No (2)＿＿＿＿＿＿＿＿ te ha quitado la fiebre?

Amiga   No lo sé, pero me (3)＿＿＿＿＿＿＿＿ mucho la garganta.

Tú   ¿Y estás (4)＿＿＿＿＿＿＿＿ algo?

Amiga   Sí, aspirina. Pero no ayuda mucho.

Tú   Vaya.

Amiga   En fin, estoy hecha una (5)＿＿＿＿＿＿＿＿.

Tú   Oye, y ¿por qué no te vas al médico?

Amiga   No, que no es nada. Ya se me (6)＿＿＿＿＿＿＿＿.

12

Special Occasions

Lola, Mark, Pepa, and Pili chat in an outdoor café.

Mark   Oye, **esta ronda es mía**...

Pepa   No, **invito yo, que es mi cumple**.

Lola   ¿Ah, sí? No lo sabía. **¡Felicidades!**

Mark   ¿Cumple? ¿Qué es eso?

Pili   Es su cumpleaños. Toma, Pepa, **esto es para ti**. (*Le da un regalo.*)

Pepa   Gracias. **¡Qué detalle!**

Pili   **Es una chorrada, pero a ver si te gusta**...

Pepa   (*Abre el regalo.*) ¡Qué dices! **¡Es genial! Me encanta**...

Mark   Pues nada, **vamos a brindar**, ¿no?

Lola   Venga. **¡Por Pepa!**

Pili   **¡Que cumplas muchos más!**

(*Todos brindan por Pepa.*)

Mark   Y **otro brindis por Lola**, para celebrar su salida del hospital.

Pili   **¡Por Lola!**

(*Todos brindan por Lola.*)

Mark   Por cierto, Lola, **te veo mejor que nunca**.

Lola   **Gracias por el piropo**...

Mark   Sí, **estás muy buena**.

Pili   Venga, **no te cortes**, Mark, dile que estás loco por ella.

Mark   Creo que ya lo sabe.

Pili   ¡Ay! ¡El amor!

Pepa   Bueno, **¡basta ya**, Pili! Escuchad todo el mundo. El sábado **hago una fiesta**. A partir de las nueve y media. **Estáis todos invitados.**

¡QUÉ DETALLE!

Mark	Hey, **this round's on me** . . .
Pepa	No, **I'm treating**, it's my *"cumple"*. (*short for* cumpleaños, *birthday*)
Lola	Really? I didn't know. **Many happy returns!**
Mark	*Cumple?* What's that?
Pili	It's her birthday. Here, Pepa, **this is for you**. (*She gives her a present.*)
Pepa	Thanks. **That's so sweet of you!**
Pili	**It's just a little something**, but I hope you like it . . .
Pepa	(*She opens the gift.*) Are you kidding! **It's great! I love it** . . .
Mark	Well, **let's make a toast**, shall we?
Lola	Yeah. **To Pepa!**
Pili	**Here's to you, kiddo!**

(*They all toast Pepa.*)

Mark	And **another toast to Lola**, to celebrate her getting out of the hospital.
Pepa	**To Lola!**

(*They all toast Lola.*)

Mark	By the way, Lola, **you're looking better than ever.**
Lola	**Thanks for the compliment.** (*literally,* flirtatious little remark)
Mark	Seriously, **you're looking really hot.**
Pili	Come on, **don't be shy**, Mark, tell her you're crazy about her.
Mark	I think she already knows.
Pili	Oh! Love is in the air!
Pepa	OK, **enough already**, Pili! Listen, everybody. **I'm having a party on Saturday.** Anytime from nine-thirty on. **You're all invited.**

Inviting

Voy a hacer...	I'm going to have . . .
una cena (bufet)	a (buffet) dinner
una fiesta (de disfraces)	a (costume) party
Estás invitad@.	You're invited. (*plural: Estáis invitad@s*)
¿Puedes venir?	Can you come?
¿Cuento contigo?	Will you come?/Can I count you in?
Me sobra una entrada para...	I have an extra ticket for . . .
Me sobran unas entradas para...	I have some extra tickets for . . .
el concierto	the concert
el teatro	the theater
¿Por qué no vienes?	Why don't you come?
¿Quieres ir?	Want to go?
¿Te apetece ir? [SP]	Feel like going?
¿Te provoca ir?☺ [LA]	Feel like going?

See also "Suggesting a Plan" on pages 14–15 in Unit 2 ("Same Time, Same Place?").

Responding
Affirmative

De acuerdo.	Alright.
Estaré sin falta.	I'll be there.
Me encantaría.	I'd love to.
Estaré, fij@.☺ [SP]	I'll be there.
Gracias por la invitación.	Thanks for the invitation.
No faltaré.	I'll be there.

Negative

Lo siento, pero...	I'm sorry, but . . .
Me encantaría, pero...	I'd love to, but . . .
no puedo	I can't
no voy a poder	I can't make it

For more ways of responding, see pages 17–19 in Unit 2 ("Same Time, Same Place?").

Playing Host

¡Me alegro de verte!	It's good to see you!
¡Qué ilusión verte! [SP]	It's great to see you!
¡Qué bien que hayas venido!	I'm so glad you've come!
¿Te apetece tomar algo? [SP]	Would you like something to eat/drink?
¿Qué te apetece tomar? [SP]	What would you like to drink?
¿Quieres...?/¿Te puedo ofrecer...?	Do you want...?/Can I offer you . . . ?
algo para picar [SP]	a little snack/a bite to eat
una copa [SP]	a drink (*alcoholic*)
un trago☺ [LA]	a drink (*alcoholic*)
un refresco	a drink (*nonalcoholic*)
Estás en tu casa.	Make yourself at home./Feel at home.
Sírvete (lo que quieras).	Help yourself (to whatever you want).
No te cortes.☺ [SP]	Don't be shy./Don't feel embarrassed.

Giving a Present

Esto es para ti.	This is for you.
Te he traído algo.	I've brought you something.
Tengo un regalo para ti.	I have a present for you.
No es nada especial.	It's nothing special.
No es nada del otro mundo.	It's no big deal.
Es una tontería.	It's just a little something.
Es una chorrada.☺ [SP]	It's just a little something.
A ver si...	I hope . . . /Let's see if . . .
te gusta	you like it
te puede servir	it'll be of use
te queda bien	it fits/suits you
Espero que...	I hope . . .
te guste	you like it
te pueda server	it'll be of use
te quede bien	it fits/suits you

Slang Flash • cortarse ☺ [SP]

This verb literally means *to cut yourself,* but in Spain, it's often used informally to mean *to feel embarrassed, awkward,* or *shy* about speaking up or doing something.

	Literal meaning	**Colloquial meaning**
No te cortes.	Don't cut yourself.	Don't be shy./Feel free.
No me voy a cortar.	I'm not going to cut myself.	I'm going to go for it.
		I'm going to be direct.
Pili no se corta nada.	Pili doesn't cut herself at all.	Pili's really outspoken.
		Pili doesn't mince her words.

Accepting a Present

(Muchas) gracias.	Thanks (a lot).
¡Qué detalle (por tu parte)!	That's so nice/sweet (of you)!
No tenías que haberte molestado.	You shouldn't have gone to the trouble.
Me gusta mucho.	I really like it.
Me encanta.	I love it.

False Friend Alert!

Yes, *un detalle* is sometimes *a detail*. But in everyday Spanish it generally means *a gesture* or *token of appreciation*.

Es un detalle. [SP]	It's a nice gesture/thought.
¡Qué detalle! [SP]	How thoughtful of you!
	That's so sweet of you!

And if someone **tiene muchos detalles**, it means they're full of little gestures and tokens of appreciation, that is, they're very thoughtful and considerate of others.

Me hace mucha ilusión. [SP]	I love it! It's great!
Es justo lo que quería.	It's just what I wanted.
¡Es divin@! ☺ [LA]	It's fabulous!
¡Es genial! ☺	It's great!
¡Es guai! ☺ [SP]	It's so cool!
¡Qué bonit@!	It's beautiful!
¡Qué lind@! [LA]	It's beautiful!

Treating

Invito yo.	It's my treat.
Deja que te invite yo.	Let me treat you.
Es mi invitación.	It's my treat/invitation.
Te invito.../Deja que te invite...	I'll treat you . . . /Let me treat you . . .
a un café	to a coffee
a una copa	to a drink
a cenar	to dinner
Esto lo pago yo.	I'm paying for this.
Esta vez me toca a mí.	It's my turn to pay.
Esta ronda la pago yo. [SP]	I'm getting this round.
Esta ronda es mía. [SP]	This round's on me.

Culture Flash • Going Bust on Your Birthday (and Saint's Day . . .)

You're in Spain and it's your birthday. But be warned before you go broadcasting it. Here the birthday boy or girl doesn't get treated, he or she *treats*. This means that if you decide to celebrate your birthday at a restaurant, you'll be expected to foot the bill, or at the very least, pay for a round of drinks after (your *amigos* will, however, give you presents, if that's any consolation). This is why Spaniards line their wallets with a few fat ones before venturing out on their birthday, or else keep it under wraps and limited to a small circle of *amigos*.

People also treat on their saints' days, which are *almost* as important as birthdays in Spain. *Saints' days*? Yes, though few Spaniards under 60 go to church regularly nowadays, everyone and his brother is named after a saint or local incarnation of the virgin. Take *Pili*, for example. This is short for *Pilar*, which is really *María del Pilar*—"Mary of the Pillar"—the pillar being a column in Zaragoza where the Virgin Mary is said to have made an apparition. Meanwhile, don't be fooled by these common nicknames (they're really saints' and virgin's names in disguise!): *Chelo* (María del Consuelo), *Concha* (María de la Concepción), *Inma* (María de la Inmaculada Concepción), *Lola* (María de los Dolores), *Kike* (Enrique), *Nacho* (José Ignacio), *Pepa* (María José), *Pepe* (José), *Paco* (Francisco), . . .

Congratulating and Wishing Well

¡Feliz año (nuevo)!	Happy New Year!
¡Feliz cumpleaños!	Happy Birthday!
¡Feliz navidad!	Merry Christmas!
¡Feliz santo! [SP]	Happy saint's day!
¡Felicidades! [SP]	Happy Birthday!/ Many happy returns!
Me alegro por ti.	I'm really happy for you.

¡Enhorabuena!	Congratulations!
¡Felicidades!	Congratulations!
¡Has hecho muy bien!	Well done!
¡Te felicito!	Congratulations! Well done!

Making a Toast

Vamos a hacer un brindis.	Let's make a toast.
¡Por...!	To . . . !
Vamos a brindar por...	Let's make a toast to . . .
Juan	Juan
los novios	the newlyweds
tu nuevo trabajo	your new job
¡Salud!	Cheers!
¡Salud, dinero y amor!	Health, prosperity, and love! (*typical toast*)
¡Que cumplas muchos más!	Here's to you! (*literally*, may you turn many more years!)

Paying a Compliment

Estás...	You look . . . /You're looking . . .
espectacular	stunning (*for women*)
muy buen@	very sexy
muy linda [LA]	very pretty/beautiful
muy guap@	really handsome/pretty
muy mon@ [SP]	very cute
radiante	radiant

Birthday Jingles

Here are two popular "Happy Birthday" songs. They're sung to the tunes of:

Happy Birthday to You	For He's a Jolly Good Fellow
Cumpleaños feliz,	Que es un/a chic@ excelente,
Cumpleaños feliz,	Que es un/a chic@ excelente,
Te deseamos todos,	Que es un/a chic@ excelente,
Cumpleaños feliz.	Y siempre lo será.

Te queda muy bien...	. . . looks really good on you.
Te favorece...	. . . is really flattering.
Te va mucho...☺ [SP]	. . . really suits you.
esa chaqueta	that jacket
ese color	that color
ese corte de pelo	that haircut

Responding

Gracias.	Thanks.
¡Qué amable eres!	That's sweet of you to say!
Gracias por el cumplido.	Thanks for the compliment.
Gracias por el piropo.*	Thanks for the coy little compliment.
¡Qué piropo!*	What a coy little compliment!
Voy a enrojecer.	I'm going to blush.

~~~~~~

Key Phrase • *te veo* + adjective

This is used a lot to compliment someone on his or her appearance, though note that in Latin America, *te ves* + adjective is more common.

Te veo muy bien. [SP]	You're looking very good.
Te ves divin@. [LA]	You look great.

Note, though, that *te veo/ves* + adjective isn't just limited to compliments. You can use it also to talk about other impressions you have of someone at a given moment.

Te veo un poco cansad@. [SP]	You look a little tired.
Te veo un poco apagad@. [SP]	You seem a little down/ out of it.

~~~~~~

---

*Note that **un piropo** is a cross between a compliment and a come-on. Note also that it's used a lot among *amigos*, even when there's zero romantic interest.

When Enough Is Enough

¡Basta ya!	That's enough!/Enough already!
¡Para ya!	Stop it!
¡No sigas!	Don't go on!/Hold it right there!
¡Ya vale!☻ [SP]	Alright already!

On the Spot

A   *Lola and Mark arrive at Pepa's party. Fill in the blanks in the conversation below.*

Pepa   ¡Hola, Lola! ¡Hola, Mark! ¡Qué bien que hayáis venido!

Mark   ¡Hola, Pepa! Oye, te (1)_____ estupenda.

Pepa   ¡Qué (2)_____! Gracias.

Lola   Es verdad, estás radiante. Mira, esto es (3)_____ ti, de los dos.

Pepa   ¡Qué (4)_____! Muchas gracias.

Lola   No es nada del (5)_____ mundo, pero a ver si te gusta. (Pepa abre el regalo.)

Pepa   ¡Es genial! Me encanta...

Mark   Me alegro.

(Lola ve a Pili y la va a saludar.)

Pepa   Oye, Mark ¿te puedo (6)_____ algo para beber? ¿Qué te (7)_____ tomar?

Mark   ¿Tienes un poco de vino?

Pepa   Claro, hay varias botellas allí. Mira, sírvete tú mismo. (8)_____ en tu casa.

B   *The party continues. Fill in the blanks in the conversation below.*

Pili   ¡Escuchadme, todos! Vamos a hacer un (1)_____.

Lola   Buena idea.

Pili   ¡(2)_____ Pepa! ¡Feliz cumpleaños!

Lola   ¡Que (3)_____ muchos más!

Pili   Venga, Pepa, no te (4)_____. Di algo.

Pepa   Pues os voy a confesar algo. Es verdad que mi cumpleaños fue el otro día. Pero hoy estoy celebrando otra cosa.

Pili   ¡Ah! Ya sé lo que es. Ha terminado el libro...

Lola   ¿Lo has terminado, Pepa? ¡(5)_____!

Mark   ¿Qué libro?

Pepa   Se llama *Spanish Among Amigos.*

Mark   Pero, ¿no escribiste eso hace unos años?

Pepa   Sí, éste es el segundo. Es un poco diferente. Más pequeño, pero más completito.

Pili   Venga, ¡vamos a (6)_____ por ese librito!

Todos   ¡Por el libro!

Lola   ¡Y por Mark, que ya habla español como un nativo!

Mark   ¡Y por mis profes! ¡Por PEPA y PILI!

Grammar Bank

Nouns

Girl or Boy?

How do you know if a noun is masculine or feminine? You can't always, but here are some rules of thumb.

Nouns are masculine if they:

1. refer to males (**el chico, el hombre, el profesor**)
2. end in *-o* or *-or* (**el libro, el amor**)
3. refer to days of the week, months, rivers, mountains, and oceans (**el lunes, el Atlántico**)

Common exceptions: *la* **mano**, *la* **flor**

Nouns are feminine if they:

1. refer to females (**la chica, la mujer, la profesora**)
2. end in *-a* (**la casa**)
3. end in *-ión, -dad,* or *-ura* (**la canción, la ciudad, la verdura**)
4. are abbreviations of feminine nouns (**la foto,** *from* **la fotografía, la moto,** *from* **la motocicleta**)

Common exceptions: *el* **día,** *el* **clima,** *el* **idioma,** *el* **mapa,** *el* **problema,** *el* **programa,** *el* **tema**

Small and/or Cute

Spanish is suffix heaven. There are loads of suffixes, and they're all juicy, as they can indicate not only size, but also the way you feel about something. The most common suffixes are the diminutive **-ito/a** and **-cito/a**. Tack these onto nouns, and presto!, you've just conveyed that something is little and/or that you're pretty fond of it. (See also "Suffix Flash" on page 85.)

mesa	table	**mesita**	small table
café	coffee	**cafecito**	coffee (*you sure do feel like having one*)
gat@	cat	**gatit@**	kitten (*and probably cute to boot*)

Meanwhile, note how adding a diminutive suffix can alter the meaning of a sentence:

Hace calor. It's *hot.*   **Hace *calorcito*.** It's *nice and warm.*

Adjectives
Agreeing and Following

Remember that adjectives agree in gender (masculine/feminine) and number (singular/plural) with the nouns they modify. Remember too that, unlike in English, they usually go *after* nouns.

un chico *alto*	a *tall* boy	**unos libros *gordos***	*fat* books
una casa *bonita*	a *nice* house	**unas calles**	*narrow*
		estrechas	streets

For using **-ísimo**, see "Cranking It Up" on page 86 in Unit 9, "Giving Descriptions."

More or Less . . .

As in English, adjectives have comparative and superlative forms.

Pepa es *más alta que* Pili.	Pepa is *taller than* Pili.
Pili es *tan lista como* Pepa.	Pili is *as clever as* Pepa.
Estos zapatos son *los más cómodos*.	These shoes are *the most comfortable.*

Comparatives and Superlatives

more . . . than	**más... que**
less . . . than	**menos... que**
as . . . as	**tan... como**
the most . . .	**el/la/l@s más...**
the least . . .	**el/la/l@s menos...**

Irregular Forms

better	**mejor**	the best	**el/la mejor, l@s mejores**
worse	**peor**	the worst	**el/la peor, l@s peores**
bigger	**mayor**	the biggest	**el/la mayor, l@s mayores**
smaller	**menor**	the smallest	**el/la menor, l@s menores**

Adverbs
(-ly) = (-mente)

To form an adverb, add -*mente* to the *feminine* form of the adjective.

rápida	*quick*	**rápidamente**	*quickly*
lenta	*slow*	**lentamente**	*slowly*

But if you're using two or more adverbs together, just add -*mente* to the last one.

rápida y silenciosa*mente*   quickly and silently

Other Ways to Go

Sometimes **con** + *a noun* is used instead of an adverb.

con **cuidado**	carefully (*literally*, with care)
con **paciencia**	patiently (*literally*, with patience)

Another common alternative is **de forma...** or **de manera...** + *an adjective.*

de forma **ilegal**	illegally (*literally*, in an illegal way)
de manera **sutil**	subtly (*literally*, in a subtle way)

As Well As

The comparative and superlative are also used with adverbs (see page 124). In this case they modify verbs, and so make comparisons about *how, when*, or *how much or how little* something is done.

Pepa habla *tanto como** Pili.	Pepa talks *as much as* Pili.
Pili cocina *tan mal como* Pepa.	Pili cooks *as badly as* Pepa.
Vente *tan pronto como* puedas.	Come *as soon as* you can.

Where and When?

Adverbs of time and place indicate where things are or when they occur.

Estoy *abajo*.	I'm *downstairs*.
El banco está *cerca*.	The bank's *nearby*.
Pili *siempre* va con prisa.	Pili's *always* in a hurry.
La película empieza *ya*.	The movie's starting (*right*) *now*.

Adverbs of Time and Place

Where?		**When?**	
abajo	down, downstairs	ahora	now
al lado	beside, next door	antes	before
		después	later
		luego	then, later
arriba	up, upstairs	nunca	never
cerca	near	pronto	soon
delante	in front	siempre	always
dentro	inside	tarde	late
detrás	behind	temprano	early
en frente	opposite	todavía	still
fuera	outside	ya	already, right now
lejos	far		

---

*Note that **tanto como** = *as much as*.

Adverbs of Manner and Quantity

How?

(muy) bien	(really) well
estupendamente	beautifully
(muy) mal	really badly
penosamente	terribly

How much?

mucho	much, a lot
(un) poco	(a) little
bastante	enough, quite a bit
demasiado	too much
suficiente	enough

Well, a Little . . .

Adverbs of manner indicate *how* something is done, and adverbs of quantity, *the degree to which* something is done.

Pili canta *muy bien*.	Pili sings *really well*.
Pepa come *demasiado*.	Pepa eats *too much*.

Useful Adverbial Phrases

a menudo	often	de vez en	from time to
a veces	sometimes	cuando	time
al fin	finally	por desgracia	unfortunately
de nuevo	again	por fin	at last
de pronto	suddenly	por suerte	fortunately
de repente	suddenly	por supuesto	of course
		rara vez	rarely

Personal Pronouns
Zap That Subject Pronoun!

Note that the subject pronoun is usually *omitted* in Spanish. This is because you don't really need it, since the verb usually makes it clear who's who.

Quiero un café.	I want a coffee.
Es de Valencia.	She's from Valencia.

But use the subject pronoun if you want to stress or emphasize the subject.

Yo **quiero un café.**	*(For example, no one else wants a coffee, but you do.)*
Ella **es de Valencia.**	*(Everyone in the group is from Madrid, except for your friend.)*

For the use of the subject pronoun in giving advice, see Grammar Flash on page 67.

Insert That Object Pronoun!

As in English, direct object pronouns are used to avoid repeating a noun previously mentioned. In most cases, direct object pronouns *precede* the verb.

¿Has visto esa película?	Have you seen that movie?
Sí, *la* **he visto.**	Yes, I've seen *it*.

¿Has terminado el libro?	Have you finished the book?
No, pero *lo* **terminaré pronto.**	No, but I'll finish *it* soon.

The Sexless *le* . . .

Indirect object pronouns say *for whom* or *to whom* an action is done. Indirect object pronouns also *precede* the verb.

Le **di el mensaje.**	I gave *him/her* the message. *(That is,* I gave the message *to him/her.)*

As you can see, the indirect object pronoun doesn't indicate the gender of the person. This is why, in order to clarify or avoid confusion, it's often accompanied by *a él* or *a ella*.

Le **di** *a ella* **el mensaje.**	I gave *her* the message.

Le la???

What if you have a direct and indirect pronoun *in the same sentence*? No problem, as long as the indirect object is **me**, **te**, **nos**, or **os**. In these cases, just string the indirect and direct pronouns (in that order) together. SO . . .

Pepa me dio el mensaje.　　　Pepa gave me the message.

becomes:

Pepa *me lo* dio.　　　Pepa gave *it* (the message)
　　　　　　　　　　　　　　　　to me.

But if the indirect object is **le** or **les**, it undergoes a little transformation and becomes **se** (to avoid the awkwardness of *le lo, le la, les lo,* or *les la*).

¿Le diste a Pili el mensaje?　　　Did you give Pili the message?
Sí, *se lo* di.　　　Yes, I gave *it to her.*

Or if, instead of a message, it was a letter (which is *feminine*: **una carta**):

***Se la* di.**　　　*I gave it* (the letter) *to her.*

Personal Pronouns

Subject	Direct Object	Indirect Object	Object after Preposition
yo	me	me	mí*
tú	te	te	ti*
él	lo	le	él
ella	la	le	ella
usted	le, la	le	usted
nosotr@s	nos	nos	nosotr@s
vosotr@s	os**	os**	vosotr@s
ellos	los	les	ellos
ellas	las	les	ellas
ustedes	les, las	les	ustedes

---

*Except with the preposition *con*: **conmigo** *(with me)* and **contigo** *(with you)* and the preposition *entre*: **entre tú y yo** *(between you and me)*
In Latin America, **ustedes and **les** are used instead of **vosotr@s** and **os**.

Possessive Adjectives and Pronouns

Possessive Adjectives		**Possessive Pronouns**	
my	**mi, mis**	mine	**mí@, mí@s**
your	**tu, tus**	yours	**tuy@, tuy@s**
his/her/its	**su, sus**	his/her/its	**suy@, suy@s**
our	**nuestr@, nuestr@s**	ours	**nuestr@, nuestr@s**
your *(pl)*	**vuestr@, vuestr@s**	yours *(pl)*	**vuestr@, vuestr@s,**
their/your *(pol)*	**su, sus**	theirs/yours *(pol)*	**suy@, suy@s**

Possessive Adjectives and Pronouns
His and Hers

One way to express possession in Spanish is using **de** (*of*).

el libro *de Pepa*   *Pepa's* book

The other way is with a possessive adjective or pronoun. Note that these agree in gender and number with the thing that's possessed and, unlike English, don't indicate the gender of the owner. That is, if the "possessed" thing is a feminine noun (for example, *una casa*), the possessive adjective or pronoun is also feminine, even if the owner is male.

Es *mi* libro.	It's *my* book.	**Es *mío*.**	It's *mine*.
Es *su* casa.	It's *his/her/ their* house.	**Es *suya*.**	It's *his/hers/ theirs*.
Son *tus* cosas.	They're *your* things.	**Son *tuyas*.**	They're *yours*.

Demonstrative Adjectives and Pronouns
Here and There

Easy: **aquí** is *here,* though note that in Latin America **acá** is more common.

Meanwhile, note that there are three words in Spanish for *there*. The differences between them are at times subtle, but basically have to do with the degree of distance from the speaker.

ahí	there (*not so far*)
allí	there (*OK, a little far*)
allá	there (*think Timbuktu*)*

This and That

Spanish also has two words for *that* and *those*. Again, the difference between them boils down to the relative distance (either in space or time) from the speaker.

ése *or* **ésa**	that one	**aquél** *or* **aquélla**	that one over there
esa **mesa**	*that* table	*aquella* **mesa**	*that* table *over there*
ese **día**	*that* day	*aquel* **día**	*that* day *way back when*

~~~~~~~~~

Demonstrative Adjectives and Pronouns

	Masculine	Feminine
this/this one	este/éste	esta/ésta
that/that one	ese/ése	esa/ésa
that/that one (*further away*)	aquel/aquél	aquella/aquélla
these/these ones	estos/éstos	estas/éstas
those/those ones	esos/ésos	esas/ésas
those/those ones (*further away*)	aquellos/ aquéllos	aquellas/ aquéllas

Note that the **e** is accented in the pronouns to distinguish them from the adjectives.

~~~~~~~~~

---

*This is not true in Latin America, where *allá* is the *there* of choice and can mean just around the corner.

Prepositions
Por or *para*?

When do you use **por** and when do you use **para**? Well, this is a little tricky, so here we'll just stick to one basic distinction:

por: what makes you do something—the *reason behind* or *cause of* your action

para: what you do something for—the *purpose* or *objective* of your action

Lo hice *por ti*.	I did it *because of you*. (*you were the cause*)
Lo hice *para ti*.	I made it *for you*. (*to give to you*)
Me fui a Roma *por amor*.	I went to Rome *for love*. (*I was in love with someone*)
Me fui a Roma *para enamorarme*.	I went to Rome *to fall in love*. (*I wanted to fall in love*)

Common Prepositions

a	to, at	**encima de**	on top of
cerca de	near	**enfrente de**	opposite
con	with	**entre**	between
contra	against	**hacia**	toward
de	of, from	**hasta**	until
debajo de	under	**para**	for, in order to
delante de	in front of		
dentro de	inside, within	**por**	for, by, through
desde	from, since	**según**	according to
detrás	behind	**sin**	without
en	in, on	**sobre**	on

Verbs
The Regular Ones

There are three types of regular verbs in Spanish: those ending in **-ar**, **-er**, and **-ir**. Tenses are formed by adding different endings to the verb stem, which is what is left of the verb once you remove the **-ar**, **-er**, or **-ir** ending. The participle (used in the *perfect* tenses) and the gerund (used in the *continuous* tenses) are also formed from the verb stem.

	-ar	-er	-ir
Infinitive	hablar	beber	vivir
	(to talk)	*(to drink)*	*(to live)*
Stem	habl-	beb-	viv-
Participle	+ado	+ido	+ido
Gerund	+ando	+iendo	+iendo

See tables of regular verbs on pages 143–145 of this section.

The Irregular Ones

The bad news is that there are lots of irregular verbs in Spanish. We can't cover them all here, but check the tables of irregular verbs starting on page 146 of this section for some of the more common ones.

Verb Tenses
Present

The present tense is used in Spanish

- to describe something happening now*

  Salgo ahora.   *I'm leaving* now.

- to express regular or habitual actions

  Pepa *lee* mucho.   Pepa *reads* a lot.

---

*You can also use the present continuous—formed by the present of **estar** + *the gerund*—to describe something that's happening now: *Estoy saliendo ahora* = *I'm leaving now.*

- to describe events that will happen in the near future

Mañana voy al dentista.   *I'm going to the dentist tomorrow.*

- to ask questions, especially ones requesting permission or someone's opinion

¿Abro la ventana?   *Shall I open the window?*

Future

The future tense is used in Spanish to talk about future events. The good news here is that the endings are the same for **-ar**, **-er**, and **-ir** verbs, and are simply tacked onto the infinitive.

Hablaré con Pepa mañana.   *I'll talk to Pepa tomorrow.*

Another way to talk about future events is using the present of **ir** + **a** + *the infinitive* (the equivalent of *to be going to* in English).

Voy a hablar con Pepa mañana.   *I'm going to talk to Pepa tomorrow.*

Past

There are three ways of referring to the past in Spanish.

- **Simple Past.** Use this to talk about completed past actions.

  Ayer llamé a Pili.   *I called Pili yesterday.*

- **Imperfect Past.** Use this to talk about past actions that went on for some time, happened repeatedly, or were going on when a completed past action (simple past) took place.

  Estaba en casa ayer.   *I was at home yesterday.*
  Pepa iba mucho al teatro.   *Pepa used to go to the theater a lot.*
  Llovía cuando salimos.   *It was raining when we went out.*

- **Present Perfect.** Use this to talk about a recent past action or one that implies a strong connection to the present. (See pages 96–97 and 99 in Unit 10, "Relaying News and Gossip," for examples of how the present perfect is used to relay news.) To form the present perfect, use the present of **haber** (*to have*) + *the past participle*.

  He terminado el libro.   *I've finished the book.*

Questions and Negative Statements
Yes/No Questions

The word order and verb stay the same. Just raise your voice at the end when it's a question. Note also that Spanish uses two question marks, an inverted one at the beginning and another one at the end.

Es alta.	She's tall.	*¿Es alta?*	*Is she tall?*
Han salido.	They've gone out.	*¿Han salido?*	*Have they gone out?*

Info Questions

The same goes for information questions as for yes/no questions. Just stick the question word in front.

¿Cuánto cuesta?	*How much does it cost?*
¿Dónde han ido?	*Where have they gone?*
¿Qué película vas a ver?	*What movie are you going to see?*

For common questions and requests, see Unit 4 ("Asking for Help or Info").

Question Words

What?	¿Qué?	Whose?	¿De quién?/ ¿De quiénes?
When?	¿Cuándo?		
Where?	¿Dónde?	Why?	¿Por qué?
Where (from)?	¿De dónde?	What for?	¿Para qué?
		How?	¿Cómo?
Where (to)?	¿Adónde?	How much?	¿Cuánto?/ ¿Cuánta?
Which one(s)?	¿Cuál?/ ¿Cuáles?		
Who?	¿Quién?/ ¿Quiénes?	How many?	¿Cuántos?/ ¿Cuántas?

Negative Statements

Just add *no* before the verb.

Pepa *no* ve la tele.	Pepa *doesn't* watch TV.
***No* salí anoche.**	I *didn't* go out last night.
***No* he estado en Grecia.**	I *haven't* been to Greece.

No-no

We come now to the infamous Spanish *double negative*. Use this when you're making a negative statement that in English would include *at all, ever, never,* or *any* (*anyone, anything, anytime, anywhere . . .*).

***No* me gusta *nada*.**	I *don't* like it *at all*.
Pepa *no* sale con *nadie*.	Pepa *isn't* going out with *anyone*.
Pili *no* ha estado *nunca* en Japón.	Pili has *never* been to Japan.

Ser vs. Estar
To be or *to be*?

Spanish has two verbs for *to be, ser* and *estar.* When in doubt, use this rule of thumb.

   Use **ser** for

- characteristics of people or things
- occupation and nationality
- telling the time

Es muy gracioso.	*He's* really funny.
Soy canadiense.	*I'm* Canadian.
Son las dos.	*It's* two o'clock.

For more examples, see Unit 9 ("Giving Descriptions").

   Use **estar** for

- temporary states (feelings, moods, physical states . . .)
- location

Estoy cansad@.	*I'm* tired.
Mi hotel está en la calle Mayor.	My hotel *is* on the calle Mayor.

For more examples, see Unit 11 ("Saying How You Feel").

For conjugations of **ser** and **estar**, see pages 146 and 149 in this section.

Watch What You Say!

Note how the meaning of these adjectives changes, depending on whether they're used with **ser** or **estar**.

ser **aburrid@**	to be *boring*	*estar* **aburrid@**	to be *bored*
ser **alegre**	to be *cheerful*	*estar* **alegre**	to be *tipsy* (drunk)
ser **buen@**	to be *good*	*estar* **buen@**	to *taste* good (food)
			to be *sexy* (people)
ser **fresc@**	to be *cheeky*	*estar* **fresc@**	to be *cool* (temperature)
ser **list@**	to be *clever*	*estar* **list@**	to be *ready*
ser **mal@**	to be *bad*	*estar* **mal@**	to be *sick*
ser **ric@**	to be *rich*	*estar* **ric@**	to be *delicious*
ser **tont@**	to be *silly*	*estar* **tont@**	to *act* silly
ser **violent@**	to be *violent*	*estar* **violent@**	to *feel* awkward/ embarrassed

Reflexive Verbs
I Myself . . .

Reflexive verbs are much more common in Spanish than English. A reflexive verb is a verb + a pronoun that refers back to the subject of the verb.

Pili *se ducha* todos los días.   Pili takes a shower (*literally*, showers herself) every day.

The tricky part: many verbs are reflexive in Spanish, but not in English. It may help to remember that many of these verbs:

1. describe actions related to personal care and daily habits
2. express feelings or changes in condition, mood or emotional state

Reflexive verbs are also used a lot in Spanish where English uses the passive voice.

Se dice que...	*It's said* that . . .
Se habla inglés.	English *is spoken*.
La película *se hizo* el año pasado.	The movie *was made* last year.

Note also the use of reflexive verbs in these common signs:

Se busca	*looking for*
Se vende	*for sale*
Se alquila	*for rent*

Reflexive Verbs

Personal Care/ Daily Habits		Feelings/Changes in Condition or Mood	
acostarse	to go to bed	aburrirse	to get bored
afeitarse	to shave	acordarse (de)	to remember
bañarse	to bathe/ to take a bath	agobiarse	to get stressed out
despertarse	to wake up	alegrarse	to be glad
dormirse	to go to sleep	desanimarse	to get discouraged
ducharse	to take a shower	divertirse	to enjoy oneself
lavarse	to wash		
levantarse	to get up	emocionarse	to get excited
peinarse	to comb one's hair	enamorarse	to fall in love
		enfadarse	to get angry
ponerse	to put on	hartarse	to get fed up
probarse	to try on (*clothing*)	motivarse	to get motivated
quitarse	to take off	olvidarse (de)	to forget
secarse	to dry off	ponerse	to become
sentarse	to sit down	preocuparse	to get worried
vestirse	to get dressed	tranquilizarse	to calm down

Conditional, Imperative, Subjunctive
Is That an Order?

As in English, the imperative is used in Spanish to give orders, instructions, or guidelines. If you're addressing one person (**tú**), use the third person singular of the simple present.*

¡Baja el volumen!	Turn down the volume!
¡Descansa!	Get some rest!

If you're addressing more than one person (**vosotros**), drop the *r* from the infinitive and add *d*. In Latin America, note that **ustedes** is used instead of **vosotros**. To form the imperative with **ustedes**, use the third person plural of the present subjunctive (see tables on pages 141 and 142 of this section).

¡Comed! [SP]	**¡Coman!** [LA]	Eat!
¡Bebed! [SP]	**¡Beban!** [LA]	Drink!
¡Sed felices! [SP]	**¡Sean felices!** [LA]	Be merry!

As for negative commands, these are always formed with the subjunctive (see "It's Unreal" on pages 140–141 of this section).

I'd Say So . . .

As in English, the conditional is used in Spanish to talk about hypothetical actions or events in the present or future. Also, like the future, the endings are the same for **-ar**, **-er** and **-ir** verbs, and are tacked directly onto the infinitive.

¿Pili se va a mudar?	Is Pili going to move (house)?
No me *sorprendería*.	It *wouldn't surprise* me.

One of the most common uses of the conditional is giving advice:

En tu lugar, lo *llamaría*.	If I were you, *I'd call* him.
Yo *no* lo *dejaría*.	I *wouldn't put* it *off*.

See Grammar Flash on page 67 in Unit 7 ("Offering Help and Advice").

---

*Irregular *tú* commands: **di** (say); **haz** (do/make), **ve** (go), **pon** (put), **sal** (leave), **sé** (be), **ten** (take), **ven** (come).

Conditional

	-ar	**-er**	**-ir**
I	hablaría	bebería	viviría
you	hablarías	beberías	vivirías
he, she, it	hablaría	bebería	viviría
we	hablaríamos	beberíamos	viviríamos
you (pl)	hablaríais	beberíais	viviríais
they, you (pol)	hablarían	beberían	vivirían

Irregular Conditional Forms

decir *(to say)*
    diría, dirías, diría,
      diríamos, diríais, dirían

haber *(to have)*
    habría, habrías, habría,
      habríamos, habríais, habrían

hacer *(to make/do)*
    haría, harías, haría,
      haríamos, haríais, harían

poder *(to be able to)*
    podría, podrías, podría,
      podríamos, podríais, podrían

querer *(to want)*
    querría, querrías, querría,
      querríamos, querríais, querrían

saber *(to know)*
    sabría, sabrías, sabría,
      sabríamos, sabríais, sabrían

salir *(to leave/go out)*
    saldría, saldrías, saldría,
      saldríamos, saldríais, saldrían

tener *(to have)*
    tendría, tendrías, tendría,
      tendríamos, tendríais, tendrían

venir *(to come)*
    vendría, vendrías, vendría,
      vendríamos, vendríais, vendrían

It's Unreal

The subjunctive crops up all over the place in Spanish. The subjunctive basically indicates *unreality, doubt,* or *desire.* But since this is pretty tricky terrain (and you don't need to be an expert on this to communicate with people), we'll just outline some of its more common uses.

Use the (present) subjunctive:

• to say you *hope* or *doubt* that something will happen

| **Espero que** *aprendas* **mucho.** | I hope you learn a lot. |
| **No creo que** *venga.* | I don't think he'll come. |

For more examples, see pages 56–57 "Expressing a Hope or Wish" and page 58, "Expressing a Negative Hope or Wish" in Unit 6 ("Wishing and Wanting") and page 115 in Unit 12 ("Special Occasions").

• in *negative* commands

No te *preocupes.*	Don't worry.
¡No os *vayáis!* [SP]	Don't leave! *(plural)*
¡No se *vayan!* [LA]!	

For more examples, see Pepa and Pili's Golden Tips on page 68 in Unit 7, "Offering Help and Advice," and Slang Flash on page 116.

• to wish someone well

| **¡Que lo** *pases* **bien!** | Have a good time! |
| **¡Que** *tengas* **buen viaje!** | Have a good trip! |

See "Little Extras" on pages 7–8.

Present Subjunctive

	-ar	-er	-ir
I	hable	beba	viva
you	hables	bebas	vivas
he, she, it	hable	beba	viva
we	hablemos	bebamos	vivamos
you (pl)	habléis	bebáis	viváis
they, you (pol)	hablen	beban	vivan

Irregular Present Subjunctive Forms

dar *(to give)*	*dé, des, dé,* *demos, deis, den*
decir *(to say)*	*diga, digas, diga,* *digamos, digáis, digan*
estar *(to be)*	*esté, estés, esté,* *estemos, estéis, estén*
haber *(to have)*	*haya, hayas, haya,* *hayamos, hayáis, hayan*
hacer *(to make/do)*	*haga, hagas, haga,* *hagamos, hagáis, hagan*
ir *(to go)*	*vaya, vayas, vaya,* *vayamos, vayáis, vayan*
poder *(to be able to)*	*pueda, puedas, pueda,* *podamos, podáis, puedan*
saber *(to know)*	*sepa, sepas, sepa,* *sepamos, sepáis, sepan*
salir *(to leave/go out)*	*salga, salgas, salga,* *salgamos, salgáis, salgan*
ser *(to be)*	*sea, seas, sea,* *seamos, seáis, sean*
tener *(to have)*	*tenga, tengas, tenga,* *tengamos, tengáis, tengan*
traer *(to bring)*	*traiga, traigas, traiga,* *traigamos, traigáis, traigan*
venir *(to come)*	*venga, vengas, venga,* *vengamos, vengáis, vengan*
ver *(to see)*	*vea, veas, vea,* *veamos, veáis, vean*

Regular Verbs
-ar Verbs

hablar (*to talk*)

	Present	Simple Past	Imperfect Past	Future
I	hablo	hablé	hablaba	hablaré
you	hablas	hablaste	hablabas	hablarás
he, she, it	habla	habló	hablaba	hablará
we	hablamos	hablamos	hablábamos	hablaremos
you (pl)	habláis	hablasteis	hablabais	hablaréis
they, you (pol)	hablan	hablaron	hablaban	hablarán

Common -ar Verbs

acabar	to finish
acercar	to bring closer/to give a lift
acompañar	to accompany
ayudar	to help
bailar	to dance
bajar	to go down
buscar	to look for
cantar	to sing
cocinar	to cook
comprar	to buy
conectar	to connect
contestar	to answer
cortar	to cut
dejar	to leave/to let
descansar	to rest
dibujar	to draw
dudar	to doubt
escuchar	to listen
esperar	to hope/to wait
estudiar	to study
explicar	to explain

fumar	to smoke
gritar	to shout
gustar	to be pleasing (*see page 45*)
hablar	to talk
limpiar	to clean
llamar	to call
llevar	to take/to wear
madrugar	to get up early
mejorar	to improve
necesitar	to need
preparar	to prepare
presentar	to introduce/to present
quedar	to stay
sacar	to take out
terminar	to finish
tocar	to touch/to play (*musical instrument*)
tomar	to take/to have (*drink or food*)
trabajar	to work
usar	to use

-*er* Verbs

beber (*to drink*)

	Present	Simple Past	Imperfect Past	Future
I	bebo	bebí	bebía	beberé
you	bebes	bebiste	bebías	beberás
he, she, it	bebe	bebió	bebía	beberá
we	bebemos	bebimos	bebíamos	beberemos
you (pl)	bebéis	bebisteis	bebíais	beberéis
they, you (pol)	beben	bebieron	bebían	beberán

Common -*er* Verbs

beber	to drink
comer	to eat
comprender	to understand
correr	to run
creer	to believe

deber	to owe
leer	to read
meter	to put in
responder	to answer
sorprender	to surprise
temer	to fear
vender	to sell

-ir Verbs

vivir (*to live*)

	Present	Simple Past	Imperfect Past	Future
I	vivo	viví	vivía	viviré
you	vives	viviste	vivías	vivirás
he, she, it	vive	vivió	vivía	vivirá
we	vivimos	vivimos	vivíamos	viviremos
you (pl)	vivís	vivisteis	vivíais	viviréis
they, you (pol)	viven	vivieron	vivían	vivirán

Common *-ir* Verbs

abrir	to open
compartir	to share
cubrir	to cover
decidir	to decide
describir	to describe
descubrir	to discover/to find out
discutir	to argue
escribir	to write
insistir	to insist
ocurrir	to happen
repartir	to distribute
subir	to go up/to climb
sufrir	to suffer
surgir	to arise/to come up
transmitir	to convey/to get across
vivir	to live

Useful Irregular Verbs

dar (*to give*)
Past Participle: (*haber*) *dado*

	Present	Simple Past	Imperfect Past	Future
I	doy	di	daba	daré
you	das	diste	dabas	darás
he, she, it	da	dio	daba	dará
we	damos	dimos	dábamos	daremos
you (pl)	dais	disteis	dabais	daréis
they, you (pol)	dan	dieron	daban	darán

decir (*to say*)
Past Participle: (*haber*) *dicho*

	Present	Simple Past	Imperfect Past	Future
I	digo	dije	decía	diré
you	dices	dijiste	decías	dirás
he, she, it	dice	dijo	decía	dirá
we	decimos	dijimos	decíamos	diremos
you (pl)	decís	dijisteis	decíais	diréis
they, you (pol)	dicen	dijeron	decían	dirán

estar (*to be*)
Past Participle: (*haber*) *estado*

	Present	Simple Past	Imperfect Past	Future
I	estoy	estuve	estaba	estaré
you	estás	estuviste	estabas	estarás
he, she, it	está	estuvo	estaba	estará
we	estamos	estuvimos	estábamos	estaremos
you (pl)	estáis	estuvisteis	estabais	estaréis
they, you (pol)	están	estuvieron	estaban	estarán

haber (*to have*)

Past Participle: (*haber*) *habido*

	Present	Simple Past	Imperfect Past	Future
I	he	hube	había	habré
you	has	hubiste	habías	habrás
he, she, it	ha	hubo	había	habrá
we	hemos	hubimos	habíamos	habremos
you (*pl*)	habéis	hubisteis	habíais	habréis
they, you (*pol*)	han	hubieron	habían	habrán

hacer (*to make/do*)

Past Participle: (*haber*) *hecho*

	Present	Simple Past	Imperfect Past	Future
I	hago	hice	hacía	haré
you	haces	hiciste	hacías	harás
he, she, it	hace	hizo	hacía	hará
we	hacemos	hicimos	hacíamos	haremos
you (*pl*)	hacéis	hicisteis	hacíais	haréis
they, you (*pol*)	hacen	hicieron	hacían	harán

ir (*to go*)

Past Participle: (*haber*) *ido*

	Present	Simple Past	Imperfect Past	Future
I	voy	fui	iba	iré
you	vas	fuiste	ibas	irás
he, she, it	va	fue	iba	irá
we	vamos	fuimos	íbamos	iremos
you (*pl*)	vais	fuisteis	ibais	iréis
they, you (*pol*)	van	fueron	iban	irán

poder (*to be able*)
Past Participle: (*haber*) *podido*

	Present	Simple Past	Imperfect Past	Future
I	puedo	pude	podía	podré
you	puedes	pudiste	podías	podrás
he, she, it	puede	pudo	podía	podrá
we	podemos	pudimos	podíamos	podremos
you (pl)	podéis	pudisteis	podíais	podréis
they, you (pol)	pueden	pudieron	podían	podrán

querer (*to want/love*)
Past Participle: (*haber*) *querido*

	Present	Simple Past	Imperfect Past	Future
I	quiero	quise	quería	querré
you	quieres	quisiste	querías	querrás
he, she, it	quiere	quiso	quería	querrá
we	queremos	quisimos	queríamos	querremos
you (pl)	queréis	quisisteis	queríais	querréis
they, you (pol)	quieren	quisieron	querían	querrán

saber (*to know*)
Past Participle: (*haber*) *sabido*

	Present	Simple Past	Imperfect Past	Future
I	sé	supe	sabía	sabré
you	sabes	supiste	sabías	sabrás
he, she, it	sabe	supo	sabía	sabrá
we	sabemos	supimos	sabíamos	sabremos
you (pl)	sabéis	supisteis	sabíais	sabréis
they, you (pol)	saben	supieron	sabían	sabrán

salir (*to leave/to go out*)
Past Participle: (*haber*) *salido*

	Present	Simple Past	Imperfect Past	Future
I	salgo	salí	salía	saldré
you	sales	saliste	salías	saldrás
he, she, it	sale	salió	salía	saldrá
we	salimos	salimos	salíamos	saldremos
you (pl)	salís	salisteis	salíais	saldréis
they, you (pol)	salen	salieron	salían	saldrán

ser (*to be*)
Past Participle: (*haber*) *sido*

	Present	Simple Past	Imperfect Past	Future
I	soy	fui	era	seré
you	eres	fuiste	eras	serás
he, she, it	es	fue	era	será
we	somos	fuimos	éramos	seremos
you (pl)	sois	fuisteis	erais	seréis
they, you (pol)	son	fueron	eran	serán

tener (*to have*)
Past Participle: (*haber*) *tenido*

	Present	Simple Past	Imperfect Past	Future
I	tengo	tuve	tenía	tendré
you	tienes	tuviste	tenías	tendrás
he, she, it	tiene	tuvo	tenía	tendrá
we	tenemos	tuvimos	teníamos	tendremos
you (pl)	tenéis	tuvisteis	teníais	tendréis
they, you (pol)	tienen	tuvieron	tenían	tendrán

traer (*to bring*)
Past Participle: (*haber*) *traído*

	Present	Simple Past	Imperfect Past	Future
I	traigo	traje	traía	traeré
you	traes	trajiste	traías	traerás
he, she, it	trae	trajo	traía	traerá
we	traemos	trajimos	traíamos	traeremos
you (pl)	traéis	trajisteis	traíais	traeréis
they, you (pol)	traen	trajeron	traían	traerán

venir (*to come*)
Past Participle: (*haber*) *venido*

	Present	Simple Past	Imperfect Past	Future
I	vengo	vine	venía	vendré
you	vienes	viniste	venías	vendrás
he, she, it	viene	vino	venía	vendrá
we	venimos	venimos	veníamos	vendremos
you (pl)	venís	vinisteis	veníais	vendréis
they, you (pol)	vienen	vinieron	venían	vendrán

volver (*to return*)
Past Participle: (*haber*) *vuelto*

	Present	Simple Past	Imperfect Past	Future
I	vuelvo	volví	volvía	volveré
you	vuelves	volviste	volvías	volverás
he, she, it	vuelve	volvió	volvía	volverá
we	volvemos	volvimos	volvíamos	volveremos
you (pl)	volvéis	volvisteis	volvíais	volveréis
they, you (pol)	vuelven	volvieron	volvían	volverán

Word Bank

This glossary is divided into 20 categories. Entries appear alphabetically in English, so you can rapidly find the word you need. Apart from key vocabulary, some categories (such as Personal Data and Telephone) also include useful phrases.

Key to Abbreviations

adj	adjective	☺	colloquial word/expression
adv	adverb	◉	soft slang
exp	phrase or expression	ⓘ	hard slang
nf	feminine noun	*sb*	somebody
nm	masculine noun	*st*	something
pl	plural (of noun)	[ACU]	Argentina, Chile, Uruguay
v	verb	[LA]	most of Latin America
@	*o/a* ending of noun	[MX]	only in Mexico
	or adjective	[SP]	only in Spain

 Arts and Leisure

Movies and Theater

actor/actress	**actor** *nm*/**actriz** *nf*
character	**personaje** *nm*
comedy	**comedia** *nf*
detective movie	**película** *nf* **policiaca**
director	**director/a** *nm/nf*
documentary	**documental** *nm*
drama	**drama** *nm*
dubbed	**doblad@** *adj*
horror movie	**película** *nf* **de terror**
love story	**historia** *nf* **de amor**
main character	**protagonista** *nm&f*
movie	**película** *nf*; [SP] **peli◉** *nf*
movie theater	**cine** *nm*
to perform/to act	**interpretar** *v*; **actuar** *v*
performance	**interpretación** *nf*
play	**obra** *nf* **de teatro**

plot	**argumento** *nm*
premiere	**estreno** *nm*
role	**papel** *nm*
scene	**escena** *nf*
science fiction	**ciencia-ficción** *nf*
screen	**pantalla** *nf*
script/screenplay	**guión** *nm*
short	**corto** *nm*
soundtrack	**banda** *nf* **sonora**
special effects	**efectos** *nm,pl* **especiales**
stage	**escenario** *nm*
subtitled	**subtitulad@** *adj*; **versión** *nf* **original**
theater	**teatro** *nm*
thriller	**película** *nf* **de miedo**
ticket	[LA] **boleto** *nm*; [SP] **entrada** *nf*
ticket office	**taquilla** *nf*

Museums and Art Exhibitions

(modern) art	**arte** *nm* **(moderno)**
art gallery	**galería** *nf* **de arte**
artist	**artista** *nm&f*
catalog	**catálogo** *nm*
exhibition	**exposición** *nf*
floor	**planta** *nf*; **piso** *nm*
hall, room	**sala** *nf*
museum	**museo** *nm*
painter	**pintor/a** *nm/nf*
painting	**cuadro** *nm*; **pintura** *nf*
permanent collection	**colección** *nf* **permanente**
sculptor	**escultor/a** *nm/nf*
sculpture	**escultura** *nf*; **talla** *nf*
work	**obra** *nf*

Music and Dance

band	**grupo** *nm*
bar/place/venue	**local** *nm*
bass player	**bajo** *nm*; **bajista** *nm&f*
composer	**compositor/a** *nm/nf*
(outdoor) concert	**concierto** *nm* **(al aire libre)**

concert hall	**sala** *nf* **de conciertos**
dance company	**compañía** *nf* **de danza**
dancer	**bailarín** *nm*/**bailarina** *nf*
drums	**batería** *nf*
guitarist	**guitarrista** *nm&f*
instrument	**instrumento** *nm*
live	**en directo** *adv*
modern dance	**danza** *nf* **moderna**
musician	**músic@** *nm/nf*
pianist	**pianista** *nm&f*
to play *(instrument)*	**tocar** *v*
program	**programa** *nm*
on tour	**de gira** *adv*
record	**disco** *nm*
show/performance	**actuación** *nf*
to sing	**cantar** *v*
singer	**cantante** *nm&f*
singer-composer	**cantautor/a** *nm/nf*
song	**canción** *nf*

 ## Bars and Nightlife

General Terms

apéritif	**aperitivo** *nm*
bar	**bar** *nm; (counter)* **barra** *nf*
bartender	**camarer@** *nm/nf*
café	**café** *nm; (outdoor café)* [SP] **terraza** *nf*
dance floor	**pista** *nf* **de baile**
discotheque	**discoteca** *nf*
drink	**bebida** *nf*
drunk	**borrach@** *adj*
glass	**copa** *nf;* **vaso** *nm*
music bar	[SP] **pub**☺ *nm;* [SP] **bar** *nm* **de copas**
party	**fiesta** *nf*
party animal	**juerguista** *nm&f;* [SP] **marchos@** *adj* and *nm/nf*
tipsy, merry	**alegre** *adj*

Drinks

(draft) beer	**cerveza** *nf* (de barril)
brandy	**coñac** *nm*
champagne	**champán** *nm*; **cava** *nm*
cocktail	**coctel** *nm*
drink (*alcoholic*)	**copa** *nf*
gin	**ginebra** *nf*
ice	**hielo** *nm*
juice	[LA] **jugo** *nm*; [SP] **zumo** *nm*
liqueur	**licor** *nm*; **aguardiente** *nm*
mixed drink	[SP] **cubata** *nm*
red/rosé/white wine	**vino** *nm* tinto/rosado/blanco
rum	**ron** *nm*
sherry	**jerez** *nm*; **fino** *nm*
shot (glass)	**chupito** *nm*
soft drink	**refresco** *nm*
whiskey	**whisky** *nm*; **güisqui** *nm*

Useful Phrases

Another round, please.	[SP] **Otra ronda, por favor.**
Excuse me!	**¡Oiga! ¡Por favor!**
How much do I owe you?	**¿Cuánto le debo?/¿Me puede decir cuánto es?**
One for the road.	**La espuela.**☺/[SP] **La penúltima.**☺

 Books, TV, and Media

Books

author	**autor/a** *nm/nf*
biography	**biografía** *nf*
(pocket) book	**libro** *nm* (de bolsillo)
bookstore	**librería** *nf*
character	**personaje** *nm*
dictionary	**diccionario** *nm*
guidebook	**guía** *nf*
library	**biblioteca** *nf*
main character	**protagonista** *nm&f*
novel	**novela** *nf*

plot	**argumento** *nm*
poetry	**poesía** *nf*
publisher	**editorial** *nf*
reading	**lectura** *nf*
short story	**relato** *nm*
textbook	**libro** *nm* **de texto**

Press

ad	**anuncio** *nm*; **publicidad** *nf*
article	**artículo** *nm*
classifieds	**clasificados** *nm,pl*
column	**columna** *nf*
correspondent	**corresponsal** *nm&f*
journalist	**periodista** *nm&f*
magazine	**revista** *nf*
monthly	**mensual** *nm*
newspaper	**periódico** *nm*; **diario** *nm*
reporter	**reporter@** *nm/nf*
review	**reseña** *nf*
reviewer, critic	**crític@** *nm/nf*
tabloid	**prensa** *nf* **amarilla**
weekly	**semanal** *nm*

TV and Radio

to broadcast	**emitir** *v*
cartoon	**dibujos** *nm,pl* **animados**
channel	**canal** *nm*; [SP] **cadena** *nf*
to channel surf [SP]	**hacer** *v* **zapping**
commercial	[SP] **anuncio** *nm*; [LA] **comercial** *nm*
documentary	**documental** *nm*
game show	**concurso** *nm*
news	**noticias** *nf,pl*; [SP] **telediario** *nm*
program	**programa** *nm*
remote control	[LA] **control** *nm* **remoto**; [SP] **mando** *nm* **a distancia**
series	**serie** *nf*
soap opera	**telenovela** *nf*; [SP] **culebrón** *nm*
to turn off	**apagar** *v*
to turn on	**encender** *v*; [LA] **prender** *v*
TV anchor/host	**presentador/a** *nm/nf*

Clothing and Accessories

Clothes

bathing suit	traje *nm* de baño; [SP] **bañador** *nm*
blouse	blusa *nf*
boot	bota *nf*
bra	sostén *nm*; [SP] **sujetador** *nm*
coat	abrigo *nm*
dress	vestido *nm*
fleece	forro *nm* polar
G-string	tanga *nm*
jacket	chaqueta *nf*
jeans	[LA] **jeans** *nm,pl*; [MX] **tejanos** *nm,pl*; [SP] **vaqueros** *nm,pl*
outfit	conjunto *nm*
panties	bragas *nf,pl*; [LA] **calzón** *nm*
pants	pantalones *nm,pl*
raincoat	gabardina *nf*; impermeable *nm*; [SP] **chubasquero** *nm*
sarong	pareo *nm*
shirt	camisa *nf*
shoe	zapato *nm*
skirt	falda *nf*
sock	calcetín *nm*; [LA] **media** *nf*
sports jacket	[LA] **casaca** *nf*; [SP] **cazadora** *nf*; [SP] **chupa** *nf*
suit	traje *nm*; [LA] **terno** *nm*
sweater	suéter *nm*; [SP] **jersey** *nm*
sweat suit	[LA] **buzo** *nm*; [SP] **chandal** *nm*
T-shirt	[SP] **camiseta** *nf*; [LA] **polo** *nm*
tights	[SP] **medias** *nf,pl*; [LA] **panties** *nf,pl*
underwear (male)	calzoncillos *nm,pl*
vest	chaleco *nm*

Accessories

belt	cinturón *nm*; [LA] **correa** *nf*
bracelet	pulsera *nf*; brazalete *nf*
brooch	broche *nm*
cap	gorro *nm*

cuff links	**gemelos** *nm,pl*
earrings	[LA] **aretes** *nm,pl*; [SP] **pendientes** *nm,pl*
glasses	[SP] **gafas** *nf,pl*; [LA] **lentes** *nf,pl*
handbag	[MX] **bolsa** *nf*; [SP] **bolso** *nm*; [LA] **cartera** *nf*
hat	**sombrero** *nm*
necklace	**collar** *nm*
ring	**anillo** *nm*; **sortija** *nf*
scarf	**pañuelo** *nm*; **bufanda** *nf* (*winter scarf*)
sunglasses	**gafas** *nf,pl* **de sol**
suspenders	**tirantes** *nm,pl*
tie	**corbata** *nf*

Clothing Fabrics and Features

brand	**marca** *nf*
button	**botón** *nm*
collar	**cuello** *nm*
corduroy	**pana** *nf*
cotton	**algodón** *nm*
fabric	**tela** *nf*
leather	**cuero** *nm*
linen	**lino** *nm*; **hilo** *nm*
pocket	**bolsillo** *nm*
rayon	**rayón** *nf*; **viscosa** *nf*
silk	**seda** *nf*
size	**talla** *nf*
sleeve	**manga** *nf*
suede	**ante** *nm*
wool	**lana** *nf*
zipper	[LA] **cierre** *nm*; [SP] **cremallera** *nf*

 # Computers and Electronics

Computers

computer	[LA] **computador/a** *nm/nf*; [SP] **ordenador** *nm*
to copy	**copiar** *v*
to delete	**borrar** *v*; **eliminar** *v*
disk	**disquete** *nm*

document	**documento** *nm*
to download	**bajar** *v*
to drag	**arrastrar** *v*
to enter	**entrar** *v*
file	**archivo** *nm*
folder	**carpeta** *nf*
hard drive	**disco** *nm* **duro**
to insert	**insertar** *v*
laptop	**portátil** *nm*
mouse	**ratón** *nm*
to move	**mover** *v*
password	**contraseña** *nf*
to paste	**pegar** *v*
to print	**imprimir** *v*
program	**programa** *nm*
recycling bin	**papelera** *nf* **de reciclaje**
to replace	**reemplazar** *v*
to save	**guardar** *v*
screensaver	**salvapantallas** *nm,pl*
to search	**buscar** *v*
search engine	**buscador** *nm*
to select	**seleccionar** *v*
server	**servidor** *nm*
tools	**herramientas** *nf,pl*
to undo	**deshacer** *v*
to update	**actualizar** *v*
warning	**aviso** *nm*
web page, website	**página** *nf* **web**
window	**ventana** *nf*
word processing	**tratamiento** *nm* **de texto**

E-mail

address	**dirección** *nf*
at (@)	**arroba** *nf*
to attach	**adjuntar** *v*
attachment	**documento** *nm* **adjunto**
dot	**punto** *nm* (*dot-com = punto com*)
e-mail	**correo** *nm* **electrónico**; [SP] **emilio**☺ *nm*
to forward	**reenviar** *v*
inbox	**bandeja** *nf* **de entrada**

outbox	**bandeja** *nf* **de salida**
to receive	**recibir** *v*
to send	**enviar** *v*

Electronics

amplifier	**amplificador** *nm*
answering machine	**contestador** *nm* **automático**
calculator	**calculadora** *nf*
cell phone	[LA] **celular** *nm*; [SP] **móvil** *nm*
charger	**cargador** *nm*
cordless telephone	**teléfono** *nm* **inalámbrico**
digital camera	**cámara** *nf* **digital**
DVD player	**reproductor** *nm* **de DVD**
ghetto blaster	**radiocasete** *nm*
headphones	**auriculares** *nm,pl*
loudspeakers	[SP] **altavoces** *nf,pl*; [LA] **parlantes** *nm,pl*
memory card	**tarjeta** *nf* **de memoria**
mini hi-fi system	**minicadena** *nf*
MP3 player	**reproductor** *nm* **MP3**
printer	**impresora** *nf*
scanner	**escáner** *nm*
stereo system	**equipo** *nm* **de música**
TV set	**televisor** *nm*
video console	**videoconsola** *nm*

 Dating and Sex

Dating

to attract	**atraer** *v*
to be in love (with *sb*)	**estar** *v* **enamorad@ (de alguien)**
to be single	**ser** *v* **solter@**
boyfriend	**novio** *nm*; **pareja** *nf*
to break up (with *sb*)	**romper** *v* **(con alguien)**
chemistry	**química** *nf*
date	**cita** *nf*
to date/to go out with (*sb*)	**salir** *v* **(con alguien)**

to fall in love (with *sb*)	**enamorarse** *v* **(de alguien)**
to flirt	**flirtear** *v*
girlfriend	**novia** *nf*; **pareja** *nf*
love at first sight	**flechazo** *nm*
to meet (*sb*)	**conocer** *v* **(a alguien)**
relationship	**relación** *nf*

Useful Phrases

Can you give me your number?	**¿Me das tu número de teléfono?**
I'd like to see you again.	**Me gustaría volver a verte.**
I'll give you a call.	**Ya te llamaré.**
Leave me alone.	**Déjame en paz.**

For common pick-up lines, see page 29 in Unit 3 ("Breaking the Ice").

Sex

affair, fling	**aventura** *nf*; [SP] **lío☻** *nm*
condom	**condón** *nm*; [SP] **preservativo** *nm*
contraceptives	**anticonceptivos** *nm,pl*
to get aroused	**excitarse** *v*
to get an erection	**tener** *v* **una erección;** [SP] **empalmarse☻** *v*
to hug	**abrazar** *v*
to kiss	**besar** *v*
to make love	**hacer** *v* **el amor;** [LA] **coger☻** *v*; [SP] **follar☻** *v*
orgasm	**orgasmo** *nm*
the pill	**la píldora** *nf*
safe sex	**sexo** *nm* **seguro**

Getting Hot and Heavy

You turn me on.	**Me excitas.**
Kiss me.	**Bésame.**
Touch me here.	**Tócame aquí.**
That feels great.	**Qué bien.**
I love it.	**Me encanta.**
Don't stop.	**No pares; Sigue.**

Please stop.	**Para, por favor.**
That hurts.	**Me estás haciendo daño.**
That was great.	**Ha sido fantástico/increíble/ maravilloso.**
Bite my . . .	**Muérdeme...**
Kiss my . . .	**Bésame...**
Suck my . . .	**Chúpame...**
Touch my . . .	**Tócame...**
breasts	**las tetas**
ear	**la oreja**
neck	**el cuello**
nipples	**los pezones**
thighs	**los muslos**

 ## Food and Meals

General Terms

breakfast	**desayuno** *nm*
to cook	**cocinar** *v*
dessert	**postre** *nm*
dinner	**cena** *nf*; [LA] **comida** *nf*
(main) dish	**plato** *nm* (**principal**)
to do the grocery shopping	**hacer** *v* **la compra**
fat (*in food*)	**grasa** *nf*
to have (*food/drink*)	**tomar** *v*
to have breakfast	**desayunar** *v*
to have dinner	**cenar** *v*; [LA] **comer** *v*
to have lunch	[LA] **almorzar** *v*; [SP] **comer** *v*
to have a snack	**picar** *v* **algo**
to have tea	**merendar** *v*
leftovers	**sobras** *nf,pl*; [LA] **restos** *nm,pl*
to set the table	**poner** *v* **la mesa**
snack/appetizer	**tentempié** *nm*; [SP] **tapa** *nf*
tea	**merienda** *nf*
to wash the dishes	**lavar** *v* **los platos**

Restaurants

check, bill	**cuenta** *nf*; **nota** *nf*
cook	**cociner@** *nm/nf*; **chef** *nm&f*
first course	**primer plato** *nm*
home cooking	**comida** *nf* **casera**
house special	**especialidad** *nf* **de la casa**
lunch special	**menú** *nm* **del día**
menu	**carta** *nf*
to order	**pedir** *v*
reservation	**reserva** *nf*
second course	**segundo plato** *nm*
server	**camarer@** *nm/nf*
(to) tip	**propina** *nf*; **dejar** *v* **propina**
wine list	**carta** *nf* **de vinos**

Food Adjectives

bitter	**amarg@** *adj*
bland/insipid	**sos@** *adj*
delicious	**ric@** *adj*; **buen@** *adj*; **delicios@** *adj*
fresh	**fresc@** *adj*
frozen	**congelad@** *adj*
heavy	**pesad@** *adj*
in season	**de temporada**
medium rare	**en su punto**
off/stale/spoiled	**pasad@** *adj*
overdone	**demasiado hech@** *adj*
rare	**poco hech@** *adj*
salty	**salad@** *adj*
sour	**agri@** *adj*
spicy	**picante** *adj*
sweet	**dulce** *adj*
well done	**bien hech@** *adj*

Getting from A to B

General Terms

to arrive	**llegar** *v*
bus station	**estación** *nf* **de autobuses**

to change (trains/buses)	**cambiar** v (**de tren/autobús**); [SP] **hacer** v **trasbordo**
coach	[LA] **autobús** nm; [SP] **autocar** nm
destination	**destino** nm
driver	**conductor/a** nm/nf
to leave/to set out	**salir** v
checkroom	**consigna** nf
lost and found	**objetos** nm,pl **perdidos**
on foot	**a pie** exp
one-way ticket	[SP] **billete** nm **de ida**; [LA] **pasaje** nm **de ida**
roundtrip ticket	[SP] **billete** nm **de ida y vuelta**; [LA] **pasaje** nm **de ida y vuelta**
subway	**metro** nm
ticket	[SP] **billete** nm; [LA] **pasaje** nm
train/bus schedule	**horario** nm **de trenes/autobuses**
train station	**estación** nf **de trenes**

Useful Terms for Directions

block	**manzana** nf (*two blocks away* = *a dos manzanas*)
corner	**esquina** nf (*at the corner of* = *esquina con*)
intersection/crossing	**cruce** nm
left	**izquierda** nf (*on the left* = *a la izquierda*)
right	**derecha** nf (*on the right* = *a la derecha*)
roundabout	**rotonda** nf; **glorieta** nf
side street	**bocacalle** nf
straight on	**todo recto** exp
traffic light	**semáforo** nm
you can't miss it	**no tiene pérdida** exp

Air Travel

airport	**aeropuerto** nm
aisle/window seat	**asiento** nm **de pasillo/ventanilla**
arrival	**llegada** nf
boarding pass	**tarjeta** nf **de embarque**
customs	**aduana** nf
departure	**salida** nf
flight	**vuelo** nm

flight attendant	**auxiliar de vuelo** *nm&f*; **azafat@** *nm/nf*
to land	**aterrizar** *v*
passenger	**pasajer@** *nm/nf*
passport control	**control** *nm* **de pasaportes**
to take off	**despegar** *v*
waiting lounge	**sala** *nf* **de espera**

Car Travel

car	**automóvil** *nm*; [LA] **carro** *nm*; [SP] **coche** *nm*
car insurance	[LA] **seguro** *nm* **de automóvil**; [SP] **seguro** *nm* **de coche**
car rental	[LA] **alquiler** *nm* **de automóvil**; [SP] **alquiler** *nm* **de coches**
to drive	[SP] **conducir** *v*; [LA] **manejar** *v*
driver's license	**carnet** *nm* **de conducir**
engine	**motor** *nm*
fine	**multa** *nf*
gas	**gasolina** *nf*
gas station	[LA] **estación** *nf* **de servicio**; [SP] **gasolinera** *nf*
gear	**marcha** *nf*
headlights	**faros** *nm,pl*
highway	**autopista** *nf*; **autovía** *nf*
highway toll	**peaje** *nm*
navigator	**copilot@** *nm/nf*
to overtake	**adelantar** *v*
to park	[SP] **aparcar** *v*; [LA] **estacionar** *v*
parking lot	[SP] **parking** *nm*; [LA] **estacionamiento** *nm*; [ACU] **playa** *nf* **de estacionamiento**
repair shop	**taller** *nm*
road	**carretera** *nf*
roadmap	**mapa** *nm* **de carreteras**
safety belt	**cinturón** *nm* **de seguridad**
speed limit	**límite** *nm* **de velocidad**
steering wheel	**volante** *nm*; [LA] **timón** *nm*
(one-way) street	**calle** *nf* **(de sentido único)**
tow truck	**grúa** *nf*
trunk	**maletero** *nm*
wheel	**rueda** *nf*

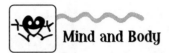

Mind and Body

General Terms

appointment	**cita** *nf*
to be on sick leave	**estar** *v* **de baja**
body	**cuerpo** *nm*; **organismo** *nm*
clinic/doctor's office	**consulta** *nf*; **consultorio** *nm*
diagnosis	**diagnóstico** *nm*
(family) doctor	**médico** *nm&f* **(de cabecera)**
emergency room	**urgencias** *nf,pl*
to heal	**curar** *v*
health	**salud** *nf*
medical checkup	**chequeo** *nm*; [SP] **revisión** *nf*
mind	**mente** *nf*
patient	**paciente** *nm&f*
to recover/to get better	**recuperarse** *v*
sick/ill (person)	**enferm@** *adj and nm/nf*
to take care of oneself	**cuidarse** *v*
X-ray	**radiografía** *nf*; **rayos** *nm,pl* **equis**

Physical Symptoms

(stomach) acidity	**acidez** *nf*
to be allergic	**tener** *v* **alergia**
to be constipated	**estar** *v* **estreñid@**
to bleed	**sangrar** *v*
blister	**ampolla** *nf*
(to) cough	**tos** *nf*; **toser** *v*
cut	**corte** *nm*; **herida** *nf*
to feel dizzy/faint	**estar** *v* **maread@**; **marearse** *v*
to feel sick/nauseous	**estar** *v* **con náuseas**
fever	**fiebre** *nf*
flu	**gripe** *nf*
to have a cold	**tener** *v* **un resfriado**; **estar** *v* **constipad@**
to have a runny nose	**tener** *v* **mocos**
high/low blood pressure	**tensión** *nf* **alta/baja**
injury	**lesión** *nf*
to lose one's voice	**estar** *v* **afónic@**
to pass out	**desmayarse** *v*

period	periodo *nm*; **regla** *nf*
to sneeze	**estornudar** *v*
to sweat	**sudar** *v*
to vomit	**vomitar** *v*; [SP] **potar☺** *v*

For more physical symptoms, see page 106 in Unit 11 ("Saying How You Feel").

Common Treatments and Remedies

bandaid	[LA] **curita** *nf*; [SP] **tirita** *nf*
bandage	**venda** *nf*
exercise	**ejercicio** *nm*
medication	**medicamento** *nm*
painkiller	**analgésico** *nm*
pill	**pastilla** *nf*; **píldora** *nf*
prescription	[LA] **prescripción** *nf*; [SP] **receta** *nf*
to rest	**descansar** *v*
stitches	**puntos** *nm,pl*
to take it easy	**no esforzarse** *v*
(physical) therapy	**terapia** *nf* (**física**)

Body Parts

ankle	**tobillo** *nm*
arm	**brazo** *nm*
ass	**culo☺** *nm*
back	**espalda** *nf*
backside	**trasero** *nm*
bone	**hueso** *nm*
cheek	**mejilla** *nf*
chest	**pecho** *nm*
chin	**mentón** *nm*
ear	**oreja** *nf*; **oído** *nm*
elbow	**codo** *nm*
eye	**ojo** *nm*
eyebrow	**ceja** *nf*
eyelash	**pestaña** *nf*
face	**cara** *nf*
finger	**dedo** *nm*
foot	**pie** *nm*
forehead	**frente** *nf*
head	**cabeza** *nf*

hip	**cadera** *nf*
knee	**rodilla** *nf*
leg	**pierna** *nf*
lip	**labio** *nm*
molar	**muela** *nf*
mouth	**boca** *nf*
muscle	**músculo** *nm*
nape of neck	**nuca** *nf*
neck	**cuello** *nm*
nose	**nariz** *nf*
palm (of hand)	**palma** *nf* **de la mano**
shoulder	**hombro** *nm*
sole (of foot)	**planta** *nf* **del pie**
stomach	**estómago** *nm*
thigh	**muslo** *nm*
thumb	**pulgar** *nm*
toe	**dedo** *nm* **del pie**
tongue	**lengua** *nf*
tooth	**diente** *nm*
wrist	**muñeca** *nf*

Money

General Terms

bill, note	**billete** *nm*
to buy	**comprar** *v*
cash	**efectivo** *nm*
(loose) change	**suelto** *nm*
cheap	**barat@** *adj*; **regalad@☺** *adj*; [SP] **tirad@☻** *adj*
coin	**moneda** *nf*
currency	**divisa** *nf*
economical	**económic@** *adj*
expenses	**gastos** *nm,pl*
expensive	**car@** *adj*
to invest	**invertir** *v*
invoice, bill	**factura** *nf*
to lend	**prestar** *v*

money	dinero *nm*; [SP] **pasta** *nf*; [LA] **plata** *nf*
to pool one's money	[SP] **poner** *v* **un fondo**
purchase, buy	compra *nf*
sale	venta *nf*
to save	ahorrar *v*
to sell	vender *v*
to spend	gastar *v*

Banking

account	cuenta *nf*
ATM	cajero *nm* **automático**
balance	saldo *nm*
check	talón *nm*; **cheque** *nm*
checkbook	talonario *nm*
commission, fee	comisión *nf*
currency exchange	cambio *nm*
debit card	tarjeta *nf* **de débito**
(to) deposit	[LA] **depósito** *nm*; **depositar** *v*; [SP] **ingreso** *nm*; **ingresar** *v*
to direct debit	domiciliar *v*
interest	intereses *nm,pl*
interest rate	tipo *nm* **de interés**
loan	crédito *nm*; **préstamo** *nm*
monthly statement	extracto *nm* **mensual**
savings	ahorros *nm,pl*
to transfer	hacer *v* **una transferencia**
to wire	hacer *v* **un giro**
to withdraw	retirar *v*

Personal Data

General Terms

age	edad *nf*
birthday	cumpleaños *nm*
date of birth	fecha *nf* **de nacimiento**
female	mujer *nf*; **femenin@** *adj*
first name	nombre *nm*
height	estatura *nf*

last name	**apellido** *nm*
male	**varón** *nm*; **masculin@** *adj*
marital status	**estado** *nm* **civil**
married	**casad@** *adj* (*to be married* = *estar casad@*)
nationality	**nacionalidad** *nf*
place of birth	**lugar** *nm* **de nacimiento**
sex	**sexo** *nm*
single	**solter@** *adj* (*to be single* = *ser solter@*)
telephone number	**número** *nm* **de teléfono**
weight	**peso** *nm*
Zodiac sign	**signo** *nm* **del Zodíaco**

Home/Residence

address	**dirección** *nf*
apartment	**apartamento** *nm*; [SP] **piso** *nm*; [ACU] **departamento** *nm*
house	**casa** *nf*; [SP] **chalé** *nm*
landlord/lady	**caser@** *nm/nf*; **propietari@** *nm/nf*
neighbor	**vecin@** *nm/nf*
neighborhood	**barrio** *nm*; **zona** *nf*
(to) rent	**alquiler** *nm*; **alquilar** *v*
room	**habitación** *nf*; **cuarto** *nm*
zip code	**código** *nm* **postal**

Nationality: See page 24 in Unit 3 ("Breaking the Ice").

Occupation: See pages 181–182 in Work (Word Bank).

Zodiac Signs

Aries	aries
Taurus	tauro
Gemini	géminis
Cancer	cáncer
Leo	leo
Virgo	virgo
Libra	libra
Scorpio	escorpión
Sagittarius	sagitario
Capricorn	capricornio
Aquarius	acuario
Pisces	piscis

Useful Phrases

Where are you from?	¿De dónde eres?
Where do you live?	¿Dónde vives?
What sign are you?	¿Qué signo eres?
How old are you?	¿Cuántos años tienes?
How tall are you?	¿Cuánto mides?
How much do you weigh?	¿Cuánto pesas?

 Physical Descriptions

Describing Things

It's . . .	Es...
dark	oscur@ *adj*
hard	dur@ *adj*
huge	enorme *adj*
light (*color*)	clar@ *adj*
light (*weight*)	liger@ *adj*
long	larg@ *adj*
modern	modern@ *adj*
new	nuev@ *adj*
old	viej@ *adj*; antigu@ *adj*
practical	práctic@ *adj*
short	cort@ *adj* (*length*); baj@ *adj* (*height*)
smooth	lis@ *adj*
soft	suave *adj*
thick	espes@ *adj*; gord@ *adj*
thin	fin@ *adj* (*of a layer or slice*)
tiny	diminut@ *adj*
useful	útil *adj*

Describing Places

It's a (very) . . . area.	Es una zona (muy)...
It's a (very) . . . place.	Es un sitio (muy)...
cheap, divey, shabby	[SP] cutre☻ *adj*
densely populated	poblad@ *adj*

elegant	**elegante** *adj*
expensive	**car@** *adj*
isolated	**aislad@** *adj*
popular/crowded	**concurrid@** *adj*
quiet/peaceful	**tranquil@** *adj*
touristy	**turístic@** *adj*
unspoiled	**virgen** *adj*
It's a (very) . . . city.	**Es una ciudad (muy)...**
It's a (very) . . . town.	**Es un pueblo (muy)...**
big	**grande** *adj*
cosmopolitan	**cosmopolit@** *adj*
expensive	**car@** *adj*
industrial	**industrial** *adj*
lively	**animad@** *adj*
modern	**modern@** *adj*
small	**pequeñ@** *adj*
ugly	**fe@** *adj*

Shopping

General Terms

bargain	**ganga** *nf*; [SP] **chollo** *nm*
cash	**efectivo** *nm*
changing/dressing rooms	**probadores** *nm,pl*; **vestidores** *nm,pl*
check-out/register	**caja** *nf*
credit card	**tarjeta** *nf* **de crédito**
customer	**cliente/a** *nm/nf*
discount	**descuento** *nm*
to go shopping	**ir** *v* **de compras; ir** *v* **de tiendas**
to haggle/bargain	**discutir** *v* **el precio; regatear** *v*
on sale	**rebajad@** *adj*
to pay (by installment)	**pagar** *v* **(a plazos)**
price	**precio** *nm*
receipt	**recibo** *nm*; **ticket** *nm*
to return	**devolver** *v*
sales	**rebajas** *nf,pl*; [ACU] **liquidaciones** *nf,pl*; [MX] **ofertas** *nf,pl*

sales assistant	**dependiente/a** *nm/nf*
size	**talla** *nf*
to stand in line	**hacer** *v* **cola**
store	**tienda** *nf*
store window	**escaparate** *nm*

For more terms, see pages 167–168 in Money (Word Bank).

Stores

bookstore	**librería** *nf*
butcher's	**carnicería** *nf*
clothing store	**tienda** *nf* **de ropa**
department store	**almacén** *nm*
drugstore	**farmacia** *nf*
fish market	**pescadería** *nf*
flea market	**mercadillo** *nm*
fruit and vegetable store	**frutería** *nf*
hardware store	**ferretería** *nf*
market	**mercado** *nm*
newspaper stand	**quiosco** *nm*
shoe store	**zapatería** *nf*
shopping center/mall	**centro** *nm* **comercial**
stationery store	**papelería** *nf*; [LA] **librería** *nf*
supermarket	**supermercado** *nm*
tobacco shop	**estanco** *nm*

 # Sports and Fitness

Health and Fitness

to be fit	**estar** *v* **en forma**
to do exercise	**hacer** *v* **ejercicio**
to do sports	**hacer** *v* **deporte**; **practicar** *v* **deporte**
to gain weight	**ganar** *v* **peso**; **engordar** *v*
to go on a diet	**ponerse** *v* **a dieta**/[SP]**régimen**
gym	**gimnasio** *nm*
healthy	**san@** *adj*; **saludable** *adj*
healthy lifestyle	**vida** *nf* **sana** (*to lead a healthy lifestyle* = *hacer* **vida** *sana*)

to join (a gym)	**apuntarse** v **a (un gimnasio)**
to lift weights	**hacer** v **pesas**
to lose weight	**perder** v **peso; adelgazar** v
outdoor sports	**deportes** *nm,pl* **al aire libre**
sportsman/ sportswoman	**deportista** *nm&f*
sportswear	**ropa** *nf* **deportiva**

Sports

baseball	**béisbol** *nm* (*to play baseball* = *jugar al béisbol*)
basketball	**baloncesto** *nm* (*to play basketball* = *jugar al baloncesto*)
boxing	**boxeo** *nm* (*to box* = *boxear*)
cycling	**ciclismo** *nm* (*to cycle* = *hacer ciclismo*)
fencing	**esgrima** *nf* (*to fence* = *hacer esgrima*)
football	**fútbol** *nm* **americano** (*to play football* = *jugar al fútbol americano*)
golf	**golf** *nm* (*to play golf* = *jugar al golf*)
handball	**balonmano** *nm* (*to play handball* = *jugar al balonmano*)
hiking	**senderismo** *nm* (*to hike* = *hacer senderismo*)
jogging	**footing** *nm* (*to jog* = *hacer footing*)
horseback-riding	**equitación** *nf* (*to go horseback-riding* = *montar a caballo*)
mountain-climbing	**escala** *nf* (*to mountain-climb* = *escalar*)
paddle tennis	**pádel** *nm* (*to play paddle tennis* = *jugar al pádel*)
sailing	**vela** *nf* (*to sail* = *hacer vela*)
scuba-diving	**buceo** *nm* (*to scubadive* = *bucear*)
skating	**patinaje** *nm* (*to skate* = *patinar*)
skiing	**esquí** *nm* (*to ski* = *esquiar*)
soccer	**fútbol** *nm* (*to play soccer* = *jugar al fútbol*)
surfing	**surf** *nm* (*to surf* = *hacer surf*)
swimming	**natación** *nf* (*to swim* = *nadar*)
tennis	**tenis** *nm* (*to play tennis* = *jugar al tenis*)
water-skiing	**esquí** *nm* **acuático** (*to waterski* = *hacer esquí acuático*)

Sports Terms

athlete	**atleta** *nm&f*
break	**descanso** *nm*
champion	**campeón** *nm*/**campeona** *nf*
championship	**campeonato** *nm*
coach	**entrenador/a** *nm/nf*
defeat	**derrota** *nf*
defense	**defensa** *nf*
foul	**falta** *nf*; [LA] **foul** *nm*
game	**partido** *nm*
goal	**gol** *nm*
to lose	**perder** *v*
overtime	**prórroga** *nf*
to play	**jugar** *v*
player	**jugador/a** *nm/nf*
race	**carrera** *nf*
score	**resultados** *nm,pl*
serve (in tennis)	**saque** *nm*
stadium	**estadio** *nm*
team	**equipo** *nm*
tennis court	**cancha** *nf*
tie	**empate** *nm*
tournament	**torneo** *nm*
umpire, referee	**árbitr@** *nm/nf*
to win, to beat	**ganar** *v*

 ## Studies and Courses

General Terms

classmate	**compañer@** *nm/nf* **de clase**
course	**curso** *nm*; **cursillo** *nm*
to enroll	**matricularse** *v*
enrollment	**matrícula** *nf*
exam	**examen** *nm*
to fail	**no aprobar** *v*; [SP] **suspender** *v*
grade	**nota** *nf*
high school	**colegio** *nm* **secundario**; [SP] **instituto** *nm*

language school	**academia** *nf*
to make progress	**avanzar** *v*
to pass	**aprobar** *v*
school	**colegio** *nm*; **escuela** *nf*; [SP] **cole☺** *nm*
school/academic year	**curso** *nm*; **año** *nm* **escolar**
to sign up (for a course)	**apuntarse (a un curso)** *v*
student	**estudiante** *nm&f*; **alumn@** *nm/nf*
teacher	**profesor/a** *nm/nf*; [SP] **profe☺** *nm&f*

College and University

bachelor's degree	**diplomatura** *nf*; **licenciatura** *nf*
college, university	**universidad** *nf*
department	**facultad** *nf*
dorm	**residencia** *nf*; [SP] **colegio** *nm* **mayor**
(oral/written) exam	**examen** *nm* **(oral/escrito)**
exchange year	**año** *nm* **de intercambio**
faculty	**profesorado** *nm*
major	**carrera** *nf*
paper	**trabajo** *nm*
Ph.D., doctorate	**doctorado** *nm*
professor	**profesor/a** *nm/nf*; **catedrátic@** *nm/nf*
research	**investigación** *nf*
subject	**asignatura** *nf*
thesis	**tesis** *nf*

College Majors and Degrees

architecture	**arquitectura** *nf*
biology	**biología** *nf*
business	**empresariales** *nf,pl*
computer science	**informática** *nf*
economics	**económicas** *nf,pl*
education	**pedagogía** *nf*
engineering	**ingeniería** *nf*
fine arts	**bellas artes** *nf,pl*
graphic design	**diseño** *nm* **gráfico**
history	**historia** *nf*
history of art	**historia** *nf* **del arte**
language and literature	**filología** *nf*
law	**derecho** *nm*

mathematics	**matemáticas** *nf,pl*
medicine	**medicina** *nf*
philosophy	**filosofía** *nf*
physics	**física** *nf*
psychology	**psicología** *nf*
social sciences	**ciencias** *nf,pl* **sociales**

 Telephone

General Terms

answering machine	**contestador** *nm* **automático**
busy	[SP] **comunica** *exp*; [LA] **ocupad@** *adj*
cell phone	[LA] **celular** *nm*; [SP] **móvil** *nm*
to dial	**marcar** *v*
to hang up	**colgar** *v*
landline	**fijo** *nm*
(cordless) phone	**teléfono** *nm* **(inalámbrico)**
to phone	**llamar** *v*; [LA] **telefonear** *v*; [SP] **dar** *v* **un toque**😊
phone call	**llamada** *nf*
phone center	**locutorio** *nm*
to pick up	**contestar** *v*; [SP] **coger** *v*
pound sign	**almohadilla** *nf*
to press	**pulsar** *v*
public phone	**cabina** *nf*
to ring	**sonar** *v*
star sign	**asterisco** *nm*
text message	**mensaje** *nm* **de texto**; **SMS** *nm*
tone, beep	**señal** *nf*

Useful Phrases

Hello.	[LA] **Aló.**/[ACU] **Hola.**/[SP] **¿Sí?/Diga.**
It's (Lola).	**Soy (Lola).**
Who is it?	**¿Quién es?**
Who's calling?	**¿Quién habla? ¿Con quién hablo?**
Hold on.	**No cuelgues.**
He'll be right there.	**Ahora se pone.**
Here he is.	**Te lo paso.**
Can I leave a message?	**¿Puedo dejar un mensaje?**

Time and Dates

Telling the Time

It's . . .	Es...
12:45	la una menos cuarto
1 o'clock	la una
1:15	la una y cuarto
1:30	la una y media
It's . . .	Son...
2 o'clock	las dos
3:30	las tres y media
7 A.M.	las siete de la mañana
8 P.M.	las ocho de la tarde
10 P.M.	las diez de la noche
4 A.M.	las cuatro de la madrugada

Useful Phrases

It's almost (one o'clock).	Es casi (la una).
It's (one o'clock) on the dot.	Es (la una) en punto.
It's just after (five).	Son (las cinco) y pico.
It's just after (six-thirty).	[SP] Son (las seis y media) pasadas.
It's five minutes to (eight).	Faltan cinco minutos para (las ocho).

Saying the Date

It's January 5.	Estamos a cinco de enero.
It's May 15, 2006.	Estamos a quince de mayo del dos mil seis.
It's July.	Estamos en julio.
It's 2006.	Estamos en el dos mil seis.

Past, Present, Future

(an hour/two days) ago	hace (una hora/dos días)
the day before yesterday	anteayer

last month/year	el mes/año pasado
last night	anoche
last week	la semana pasada
a while back	hace tiempo
now, currently	actualmente
nowadays	hoy en día
right now	ahora mismo
the day after tomorrow	pasado mañana
in (ten minutes/ a week)	dentro de (diez minutos/una semana)
in a little while	dentro de un rato
next month/year	el mes/año que viene
next week	la semana que viene

Other Time Expressions

(tomorrow) morning	(mañana) por la mañana
(Monday) afternoon	(el lunes) por la tarde
(Friday) night	(el viernes) por la noche
in early (August)	a principios de (agosto)
in mid-(October)	a mediados de (octubre)
in late (January)	a finales de (enero)
in the first two weeks of (April)	en la primera quincena de (abril)
in the last two weeks of (July)	en la segunda quincena de (julio)
in the sixties	en los años sesenta
in the (19th) century	en el siglo (diecinueve)
in the Middle Ages	en la edad media
in the Stone Age	en la edad de piedra

 Vacations and Travel

General Terms

backpack	mochila *nf*
baggage, luggage	equipaje *nm*
day trip	excursión *nf*
to go sightseeing	visitar *v* la ciudad; ver *v* los monumentos

guide	**guía** *nm&f*
high/low season	**temporada** *nf* **alta/baja**
historic center	**casco** *nm* **antiguo**
holiday	**día** *nm* **festivo**
to pack	**hacer** *v* **las maletas**
package trip	**viaje** *nm* **organizado**
tourist office	**oficina** *nf* **de turismo**
to travel	**viajar** *v*
travel agency	**agencia** *nf* **de viajes**
trip	**viaje** *nm*
vacation	**vacaciones** *nf,pl*
weekend	**fin** *nm* **de semana**; [SP] **finde☺** *nm*

For transportation, see pages 162–164, Getting from A to B (Word Bank).

Hotels and Hostels

to book	**reservar** *v*
hostel	**hostal** *nm*
hotel	**hotel** *nm*
key	**llave** *nf*
room	**habitación** *nf*
rural B and B	**casa** *nf* **rural**
to stay *(as in hotel)*	**estar** *v* **hospedad@**; **estar** *v* **alojad@**
youth hostel	**albergue** *nm* **juvenil**

Camping

to camp	**hacer** *v* **acampada**
campsite	**camping** *nm*
flashlight	**linterna** *nf*
mat	**colchoneta** *nf*; **esterilla** *nf*
penknife	**navaja** *nf*
sleeping bag	**saco** *nm* **de dormir**
tent	**tienda** *nf* **(de campaña)**
washing facilities	**instalaciones** *nf,pl*

Beach Bumming

beach	**playa** *nf*
beach bar/restaurant	[SP] **chiringuito** *nm*; [LA] **quiosco** *nm*
cove	**cala** *nf*
to get burned	**quemarse** *v*
to get tan	**broncearse** *v*

lifeguard	**socorrista** *nm&f*
parasol	**sombrilla** *nf*
sand	**arena** *nf*
sea	**mar** *nm*
to sunbathe	**tomar** *v* **el sol**
sunblock	**crema** *nf* **solar**
to take a dip	**darse** *v* **un baño**; [SP] **pegarse** *v* **un baño**
(high/low) tide	**marea** *nf* **(alta/baja)**
towel	**toalla** *nf*
wave	**ola** *nf*

 Weather

The Basics

How's the weather?	**¿Qué tiempo hace?**
It's . . .	**Hace...**
chilly	[SP] **fresquito** *adj*
cold	**frío** *adj*
cool	**fresco** *adj*
(twenty) degrees	**(veinte) grados** *nm,pl*
good weather	**buen tiempo** *nm*
hot	**calor** *nm*
muggy	[SP] **bochorno** *nm*
sunny	**sol** *nm*
windy	**viento** *nm*; **aire** *nm*

General Terms

climate	**clima** *nm*
cloudy	**nublad@** *adj*
drizzle	**llovizna** *nf*
drought	**sequía** *nf*
dry	**sec@** *adj*
fog	**niebla** *nf*
hail	**granizo** *nm*
humid	**húmed@** *adj*
mild	**suave** *adj*
overcast	**cubiert@** *adj*

(to) rain	**lluvia** *nf*; **llover** *v*
(to) snow	**nieve** *nf*; **nevar** *v*
storm	**tormenta** *nf*; **borrasca** *nf*

Useful Phrases

It's pouring.	**Está diluviando.**☺/**Llueve a cántaros.**☺/ [SP] **¡La que está cayendo!**☺
It's so cold!	**¡Qué frío!**
It's so hot!	**¡Qué calor!**
It's so humid!	**¡Qué húmedo!**
It's so windy!	**¡Qué viento!**

Work

General Terms

to be unemployed	**estar** *v* **sin trabajo**; [SP] **estar** *v* **en paro**
boss	**jefe** *nm*/**jefa** *nf*
business trip	**viaje** *nm* **de negocios**
colleague/office mate	**compañer@** *nm/nf* **de trabajo**
company	**empresa** *nf*; **compañía** *nf*
employee	**emplead@** *nm/nf*
family business	**negocio** *nm* **familiar**
to hire	**contratar** *v*
to lay off	**despedir** *v*; [SP] **echar** *v*
meeting	**reunión** *nf*
office	**oficina** *nf*; **despacho** *nm*
partner	**soci@** *nm/nf*
project	**proyecto** *nm*
salary	**salario** *nm*; **sueldo** *nm*; [SP] **nómina** *nf*
team	**equipo** *nm*
to work	**trabajar** *v*; [SP] **currar**☺ *v*
work	**trabajo** *nm*; [SP] **curro**☺ *n*
work day	**horario** *nm*; **jornada** *nf* **laboral**

Professions

accountant	**contable** *nm&f*
archaeologist	**arqueólog@** *nm/nf*
architect	**arquitect@** *nm/nf*

auditor	**auditor/a** *nm/nf*
biologist	**biólog@** *nm/nf*
cabdriver	**taxista** *nm&f*
carpenter	**carpinter@** *nm/nf*
civil servant	**funcionari@** *nm/nf*
computer scientist	**informátic@** *nm/nf*
construction worker	**albañil** *nm&f*
dentist	**dentista** *nm&f*
designer	**diseñador/a** *nm/nf*
doctor	**médico** *nm&f*; **doctor/a** *nm/nf*
electrician	**electricista** *nm&f*
engineer	**ingenier@** *nm/nf*
entrepreneur	**empresari@** *nm/nf*
factory worker	**obrer@** *nm/nf*
farmer	**agricultor/a** *nm/nf*
firefighter	**bomber@** *nm/nf*
freelancer/ self-employed	**autónom@** *nm/nf*
homemaker	**am@** *nm/nf* **de casa**
journalist	**periodista** *nm&f*
lawyer	**abogad@** *nm/nf*
mechanic	**mecánic@** *nm/nf*
nurse	**enfermer@** *nm/nf*
painter	**pintor/a** *nm/nf*
photographer	**fotógraf@** *nm/nf*
physicist	**físic@** *nm/nf*
plumber	[SP] **fontaner@** *nm/nf*; [ACU] **plomer@** *nm/nf*
psychologist	**psicólog@** *nm/nf*
scientist	**científic@** *nm/nf*
secretary	**secretari@** *nm/nf*
teacher	**profesor/a** *nm/nf*
translator	**traductor/a** *nm/nf*
waiter/server	**camarer@** *nm/nf*
writer	**escritor/a** *nm/nf*

Common Idioms and Expressions

¡A por ello!☺ *exp*
Go for it!

¡A saber!☺ *exp*
Who knows? Your guess is as good as mine.

aburrirse *v* como una ostra☺
to be bored to tears

actuar *v* como si nada☺
to play it cool; to act like nothing's happened

aguafiestas *nm&f*
killjoy or party pooper

Algo es algo.☺ *exp*
It's better than nothing.

andar *v* en las nubes☺
to be on cloud nine; to be daydreaming

aprovecharse *v* (de algo)
to take advantage (of *st*) (*can be positive or negative*)

una barbaridad *nf*
1) a lot (of *st*) 2) a terrible, daring, or crazy act

cachondeo☺ *nm*
having fun; horsing around

cachond@☺ *adj* [SP]
(*with ser*) funny; (*with estar*) excited, horny

coger *v* el toro por los cuernos [SP]
to take the bull by the horns

como Dios manda☺ *adv*
properly, correctly (*literally, as God dictates*)

costar *v* (trabajo)
to be very difficult; to be a big effort

costar *v* un dineral☺
to cost a fortune

costar *v* un ojo de la cara☺
to cost an arm and a leg

cueste lo que cueste *adv*
come hell or high water

dar *v* ánimos (a alguien)
to encourage (*sb*); to give (*sb*) moral support

dar *v* la lata (a alguien)☺
to bother/pester/bug (*sb*)

darse *v* cuenta de (algo)
to realize or notice (*st*)

dar *v* una vuelta
to go for a walk or ride

echar *v* un vistazo (a algo)
to take a look (at *st*)

echar(le) *v* leña al fuego☺
to add fuel to the fire

183

estar *v* a punto (de hacer algo)	to be just about (to do *st*)
estar *v* al loro☻ [SP]	to be alert/to be up on *st*
estar *v* chupado☻ [SP]	to be a cinch/piece of cake
estar *v* como un tren☻ [SP]	to be "hot"/a hunk (*of men*)
estar *v* en camino	to be on one's way
estar *v* en la ruina☺	to be broke
estar *v* forrad@☻	to be loaded/very wealthy
estar *v* mal de dinero☺	to be hard up
estar *v* sin un duro☺ [SP]	to be flat broke
estar *v* sin plata☻ [LA]	to be broke
estar *v* rendid@	to be exhausted/worn out
gorrón/gorrona☻ *adj and nm/nf*	leech, freeloader
gorronear☻ *v*	to mooch off (*sb*)
una gozada☺ *nf* [SP]	great, wonderful, a real treat
guardar *v* las apariencias	to keep up appearances
hacer(se) *v* a la idea	to get used to the idea
hacer(se) *v* el/la interesante☺	to play hard to get
hacer *v* las paces☺	to call it quits; to bury the hatchet
hacer *v* la pelota☺	to brownnose; to kiss ass
ir *v* de compras/tiendas	to go shopping
ir *v* de mal en peor	to go from bad to worse
ir *v* volando☺	to rush off
jugar(sela) *v*	to take a risk or a chance
mala leche☻ *nf*	malice
meter(le) *v* mano a (alguien)☺	to feel (*sb*) up
meterse *v* con (alguien)☺	to mess with (*sb*); to look for trouble with (*sb*)
montar *v* un número☻	to make a scene
no dar *v* ni golpe☺	to sit around doing nothing; to be idle
no dar *v* una☺	to be completely inept; to do everything wrong
No es para tanto.☺ *exp*	It's not that big of a deal.
no pegar *v* ojo☺	not to sleep a wink

¡No te pases!☺ *exp*	Don't push your luck!/ Don't get smart!
pagar *v* una fortuna☺	to pay a fortune
partirse *v* (de risa)☻	to crack up (laughing)
pasarlo *v* bomba☻/[SP] pipa☻	to have a blast/great time
pase lo que pase *adv*	come what may; whatever happens
pez *nm* gordo☺	big shot, bigwig
poder *v* con (algo/alguien)☺	to be able to cope with (*st/sb*)
ponerse *v* las pilas☻	to get on the ball
¡Qué mala pata!☺ *exp*	What a bummer! That was bad luck!
quedarse *v* boquiabierto☺	to be dumbfounded
quedarse *v* frit@☻	to fall asleep
¿Qué más da?☺ *exp*	So what? Who cares?
rajar(se)☻ *v*	[MX] to go back on your word; [SP] to back out (of a plan)
salirse *v* con la suya☺	to get one's way
ser *v* la gota que colma el vaso☺	to be the last straw
sin rodeos *adv*	without beating around the bush
tal cual *adv*	as is; just as it is
tener *v* buena pinta☺	to look good or appealing
tener *v* cara☺	to be cheeky; to have nerve
tener *v* chispa☺	to have "spark"; to be fun/lively/witty
tener *v* cojones/huevos☻ [SP]	to have (a lot of) guts/balls
tener *v* (algo) en cuenta	to keep (*st*) in mind; to take (*st*) into account
tener *v* morro☻ [SP]	to have nerve (*in the negative sense*)
tener *v* prisa	to be in a hurry
tener *v* sentido	to make sense
un timo☺ *nm*	a rip-off
tipej@☺ *nm/nf*	louse; unsavory character
tirar *v* el dinero☺	to waste money

tirar *v* **la casa por la ventana**☺	to go all out; to splurge
¡Trato hecho! *exp*	It's a deal!
un montón☻ *adv*	a lot
valer *v* **la pena**	to be worth it
Vamos bien. *exp*	So far, so good.
¡Ya caigo!☺ [MX/SP] *exp*	Now I get it!
Ya está. *exp*	That does it./That's that.

Answer Key

1 Meeting and Greeting

A 1. tal   2. vida   3. novedades   4. está   5. siglos   6. parte
7. vemos   8. Hasta

B 1. bien   2. cuánto   3. presento   4. tal   5. gusto   6. vaya
7. día   8. Hasta

2 Same Time, Same Place?

A 1. tienes   2. apetece *or* provoca   3. quedamos   4. viene
5. siempre   6. apuntas   7. conmigo

B 1. quedar   2. preocupes   3. Es que   4. pasa   5. dejamos
6. importa

3 Breaking the Ice

A 1. fuego   2. american@, inglés/inglesa, etc.   3. llevas
4. conoces   5. hace   6. toda   7. desde

B 1. eres   2. trabajas   3. dedicas   4. haces   5. Soy
6. digas   7. tomando

4 Asking for Help or Info

A 1. llama   2. prestas *or* dejas   3. Toma   4. escribe
5. dice   6. pedir   7. prestas *or* dejas   8. no

B 1. hora   2. Perdón, Perdona, Cómo, *or* Qué (has dicho)
3. entendido *or* captado   4. hora   5. lejos

5 Likes and Dislikes

A 1. gustas   2. gusta   3. bien   4. gracia   5. cae *or* cayó
6. parece

B 1. gusta   2. dice   3. encanta, apasiona, fascina, *or* chifla
4. horror *or* espanto   5. nada   6. loc@

6 Wishing and Wanting

A 1. encantado   2. apetece, provoca, gustaría, *or* encantaría
3. sí   4. deseando   5. ganas   6. paso   7. nada

B 1. Tenías   2. hubiera   3. ganas   4. importaría
5. perdiste   6. quedé

7 Offering Help and Advice

A 1. me   2. iría   3. puedes   4. consejo *or* recomendación
5. tú   6. bien
B 1. qué   2. no   3. fuera *or* fuese   4. te   5. caso
6. arrepentir

8 Speaking Your Mind

A 1. opinas *or* piensas   2. parece   3. digas   4. mí   5. duda
6. Estoy
B 1. gusta   2. parece *or* resulta   3. Pesado   4. Qué
5. crees   6. idea

9 Giving Descriptions

A 1. personaje   2. simpática   3. divertida   4. extravagante
5. atención   6. graciosa
B 1. cariñoso *or* cálido   2. independiente   3. inquieta
(feminine, to agree with "persona")   4. bajo *or* bajito
5. gordo *or* gordito   6. atractivo

10 Relaying News and Gossip

A 1. oído   2. enterado   3. idea   4. horror   5. visto
6. mal   7. Vaya
B 1. lo   2. nada   3. creo   4. acaban   5. Qué   6. parece
7. pierdas

11 Saying How You Feel

A 1. encuentras   2. grave   3. me   4. pasado   5. tiene
6. Está
B 1. estás   2. se   3. duele   4. tomando   5. pena
6. pasará

12 Special Occasions

A 1. veo   2. piropo   3. para   4. detalle   5. otro   6. ofrecer
7. apetece   8. Estás
B 1. brindis   2. Por   3. cumplas   4. cortes
5. Enhorabuena *or* Felicidades   6. brindar